CW00347144

HOCKEY

A Philosophical Game

Andreu Enrich

To those who doubt

Contents

PROLOGUE

Philosophizing with a Hammer

What is hockey? Why do we win? What is to succeed? What is to play well? And playing nice? Why do we train? What should we practise? What should we do as coaches? Why should we try to improve our players? What is to have a good team? Why do we need a style of play?

Philosophy (literally "love of wisdom") is the art of making questions. It is a different way of thinking, a way that puts us more in trouble, a way of thinking that disturbs and makes us feel insecure. Philosophy aims to reach the deep meaning of the things. And once something is achieved, that certainty is discarded and philosophy brings us further and further. Philosophy is essentially the art of doubting. Its main target is to doubt about those aspects that we take for granted. To doubt about the obvious.

Every discipline, every field of knowledge, every event is subjected to be approached by philosophy. Philosophers started to focus on life, the world, god, the evil, humans, reason, mind, language... but the interest of philosophers also reached other fields of the social sphere like politics, art, love, science, technology, education, economy and also sport.

Today we can find thousands of papers, books and documentaries about sport. The rise of professional sport in our society attracted best experts from other disciplines, a fact that turned sport into a very broad field of knowledge. Science has been deeply engaged, bringing theories and studies about how to maximize performance. Psychologists also have become relevant in the understanding and management of the emotions and the mental health of our athletes. Technology arrived with tones and tones of data, trying to track every single phenomenon of our practise. And even marketing gurus approached sport and tried to convert our players into social icons. But what about philosophers?

In sport, what can we get in return from philosophers?, you will be tempted to pose. And a philosopher would reply: why should we always get something in return? Indeed, philosophy is a way of thinking that doesn't provide any easy and cheap answer. From this point of view, philosophy has no practical utility itself. Are we "philosophizing" enough in sport, and especially in hockey?

Hockey is a big small world. People from hockey have never been so interested in sharing deep thoughts with others. On the internet you can find hundreds of papers about hockey performance. Hundreds of books and videos about training methodologies, drills and even about weird hockey tricks. There are very few books about famous hockey personalities with their views and experiences, like Ric Charlesworth and his "World's Best". I think we need more testimonials from great athletes and coaches. But if we talk about more conceptual or abstract contents, the list tends to zero. And it is not that we don't have enough thinkers in hockey, of course. We have lots of them! But it seems that we never found this divulgation activity interesting enough to justify something longer than a couple of tweets.

In my personal case, I'm naturally inclined about philosophy and its vices. I can't help it anymore. One of these vices is to write. Although I love to read, I can survive without books. But I can't make it without writing. My mind is constantly flying away while exploring different ideas and concepts, but when it comes back it demands me to put these thoughts into a blank paper. Since the last three years I've been producing various texts about hockey. Texts that were emerging, expressed, published and forgotten in time.

In the present book you will find the result of these philosophical reflections: a compilation of 33 texts . This compilation is the result of what I've written in the past three years. All the texts have been updated, reviewed, corrected and adapted.You will find a bit of everything. There are some about hockey events, umpires, formats and officials; texts about clubs, managers, coaches and players. There are just purely abstract reflections but also more concrete proposals. Texts inspired in famous philosophers, scientists, artists and coaches from other disciplines. You will find texts about the past, present but also about the future.

But besides this heterogeneity you will find something common: a will to provoque. Nietzsche said that we should philosophize with a hammer. To be brave, straight, provocative and disruptive appear as something really important to me when thinking and reflecting about hockey. Take my arrogance as an invitation and try to demolish every reflection with the hammer of your reason. Take it as a kind of game, because it's fun!

I hope you find this book stimulating, attractive, interesting and useful. In that order.

Goal hug,

Andreu

TOURNAMENTS

Reflections after the Champions Trophy 2018

02/07/2018

What have been the main developments in gameplay since Rio2016?

The main development in gameplay since Rio has been the boom of direct play. This new trend can be partly because of the Argentinian success using this style of play in the last Olympics. This direct play can be easily confirmed while attending the number of aerials per game and the number of long crosses played into the circle. Today almost every good player in the world must dominate aerials, from Ibarra to Luypaert, from Baart to Zalewski. I'm not only talking about long aerials, also short ones that have been used as a resource to just eliminate one line (especially with the rule of "5-meter distance" that creates a safe area for the receiver). If in WC 2014 the aerial goal from Knowles to Govers was something that has never been seen before, these types of actions are much more common now.

It has happened the same with the blind balls thrown inside the circle (aka hit & hope) . Argentina was exploiting this resource during RIO with the perfect ambassador Lopez. These days almost all the teams are playing long balls inside the circle after crossing the middle line. Crossing and hoping that inside the circle, due to strong 1v1's physical contests, someone will be able to receive the ball or deflect it. Unpredictability in its purity.

What are the technical, tactical & behavioral highlights you have observed at HCT2018?

From the 1st day of the tournament we have seen how the tactical trend in defense has been the zonal system. From my skeptical point of view there are no rational arguments that can justify this trend (trends are not always rational). I claim that the pure zonal is condemned to fail in the near future. And basically for three main reasons:

1) The use of quick re-starts makes the defensive overloads very risky in case of free hit achieved by the attacker.

2) The aerials inside the boxes can't be defended and the aerials above the zone are difficult to cover as well.

3) The switch from zonal to man2man in your own half. We've seen many teams killing the opponent with diagonal passes from the side to the top of the circle (to the post-up) after crossing the midline.

Another aspect I've seen during this tournament is the massive use of the post-up role. In almost every attacking situation there is a post-up man dropping from the depth, receiving with good body protection and waiting for the 2nd wave players to arrive or, if his position is inside the circle, looking for a shielding progression and then a backward shot. This combinatorial game that takes place in the vertical axis is the basement of a good progression, and I love it. What I have not seen during this event is a lot of 1v1 eliminations. Most of the players when they are facing an opponent they tend to fall into the conservative decision to protect the ball with the body and turn. How many times have we heard an "ohhhh" from the stands after a nice 1v1 elimination? Very few.

What changes would you make to your game analysis approach in order to provide more useful information for you and your team?

I think that the way we analyze the games is becoming obsolete. What does a typical game analysis look like? Outlets, presses, circle entries, set pieces…. That is like having a scientist trying to explain the secrets of a good samba dancer. First of all: games are living entities with flows and phases. The momentum is something that we must take into account when we analyze a game. Depending on the game momentum we will have to respond in a different way. Is the same offensive transition context if we are losing or winning? Is the same transition if we previously had 3 quick ball losses? Is the same transition if Herzbruch regains the ball than if it is Matania? Our tactical analysis doesn't take this complexity into consideration yet. Momentum Analysis is the future.

The other area that we should attend in our analysis is the individual decision-making of our players. That means perception (analyze the quality & quantity of the vision of the player), decision (significant stimulus perceived) and execution (skill chosen, skills errors). Briefly, less "macro" structures and events and more individual and complex situations.

What are the main "grey" areas in interpretation & application of the rules of hockey?

Hockey is grey. There is too much room for interpretation. The main problem in our sport is how to control the danger. But danger is something subjective, and this is problematic. How dangerous is a high ball inside the circle? How dangerous is a 1v1 physical contest? How dangerous is receiving that aerial? How dangerous or deliberated is a physical push?

In my opinion, the most important discussion now is how to regulate the aerials because the rule is counter-intuitive. Despite that rule, I like the high degree of tolerance that umpires are showing towards tackles and physical duels. The fewer offenses we can have in the game the more attractive for spectators hockey will be. Are we blowing fewer faults per game now than in Rio? That could be a good KPI to consider (and try to reduce) for the umpires.

How can we (as HP coaches) contribute to future development and interpretation of the rules of hockey?

We need constant and fluent communication between bodies. There must be a panel of top coaches in relation with top umpires that meet regularly for discussions about the fundamentals of the game and the rules. Rules and game style must evolve together.

Joint analysis of controversial decisions, shared data about the faults umpired, etc. What data and what type of analysis are the umpires using?

What innovations in game-play will we see from now to Tokyo2020?

Free-man as a function: not as a position: defensive systems will be based on constant and organic adjustments. We might always find someone free, but this person will always be different, depending on the situation. No predefined man2man or zonal system. The hegelian synthesis is around the corner. It will be seen quite chaotic from outside, but it is precisely this unpredictability for the opponent that will be the key to its success. Australia in 2014, Argentina in 2016, and bring it to the extreme.

Multifunctional players: Constant interchanges. In the future it will make no sense to ask in what position Valentin Verga or Arthur Van Doren play. The team that creates more multifunctional players first will be the first team to perform above the others and probably win the next World Cup and Olympics. The more we focus on patterns, mechanisms, and positions, the worse. The more we focus on principles, the better. The key is to deconstruct the complexity of the game in some fundamental principles that can guide any player in understanding how to play. If we as coaches provide the right interpretative tools to the players, they will be ready to perform under any situation.

My World Cup "Dream Team"

20/12/2018

The World Cup is over in India. It's been three weeks of great fun, enjoying our sport with the best possible display. Congrats to the organization and to all the sponsors who made it possible. Congrats to Belgium as well, you guys finally have tasted the flavor of the victory, very well deserved! Let's see if you are able to keep the same level of hunger until Tokyo.

In this tournament we've seen a bit of everything: disappointing top teams, disappointing poor teams, consistent teams with a lack of goal, dangerous teams with lack of consistency, revelation teams, teams in the building process towards Tokyo and teams in the process of Mordor.

In the present text I want to show my "Dream Team" of the WC. To judge the quality of something is a pure subjective act, also with hockey players. So this Dream Team contains a lot of me and my hockey taste, of course. Here we go:

Pirmin Blaak: *Rocky II*. Pirmin has been orbiting around the goalkeeper spot of the Oranje for many years but he had to face Jaap Stockman in that process, which is a big thing. Never giving up (he was injured some weeks before the tournament) and patiently waiting for his opportunity: to be the main goalie in a major tournament. The chance arrived at 30 years-old and he showed his best version. Let's hope that he can keep this top level until the Olympics. *"Gonna fly now"* is his song.

Jonas de Geus: *The pirate of Almere.* Jonas is a post-modern player. He can play anywhere across the field. Good spatial awareness and smooth technique. Long arms that allow him to carry the ball far from the defender but always under control. Jonas has made a very good tournament in general. I say "in general" because he's still young and has committed some "bad boy" mistakes. However, this is something that will naturally disappear after playing more caps.

Gauthier Boccard: *The threatened Swan (from Asselijn).* Another player that made a significant step in this tournament. Gauthier has been in the Belgium squad since London 2012. But it has been now, with 27 years-old, when he has exploded and shown all of his potential. Another all-rounded player. These days he plays as right and left back but he could play anywhere else without a problem. He dominates all the possible skills, including the hit as a long fake pass which is difficult to find these days. He's still better than what he showed in this tournament.

Harmanpreet Singh: *The golden stick from Amritsar.* If there is only a single indian player in my dream team squad, you would never expect a defender right?. But yes, I've chosen Harmanpreet.

This guy is a top drag flicker, but he is not only a drag flicker. He performs well in long aerial passes, fake sweeps and also using the powerful asian hit. But that's not all, under pressure he has shown good skills and also the capacity to dribble and progress with the ball under control. And he is still young!

Arthur van Doren: *De Leeuw.* There is something more important than being one of the best players in the world: to be unconsciously recognized by your opponents as one of them. Arthur possesses this special aura. The Lion King. He has this presence inside the field, this special self-confidence that goes beyond the ordinary and blinds others. He can lose balls, throw a melon as a pass or concede some easy corners against. But his presence always remains intact. He is one of the best players in the world, but out of them he is the only one who hasn't reached his potential yet.

Hugo Genestet: *Didier Deschamps.* Give me 11 Genestet -including brothers, cousins and nephews- and I will become invincible. The smartest guy of the class. He is not the strongest, nor the fastest, nor the most skillful, but he is one of the best players, why? Because he understands the game better than the majority, so he's able to rule the game according to his will. He doesn't run any stupid meter in the whole game. A great example of smart decision-making and economic effort.

David Ames: *Adam Clayton.* David is the bass of England, the one who sustains the whole song while managing the rhythm of the game. Every team needs one Sergio Busquets. Very important role in the midfield, always providing an easy short option and always ready to find the next one. Good vision skills, awareness of the close and distant teammates and able to keep calm under stressed situations. David is the perfect metronome of my Dream Team.

Mats Grambusch: *e-Golf.* Yes, he is a Volkswagen but he is electric. The old and the new. The new paradigm of hockey player within a traditional german structure. The Hegelian synthesis is here. Germany is in the process of Tokyo, finding and defining its new identity. Mats is a wise guy with a huge potential for leadership and really good in combining verticality with control.

Billy Bakker: *Old Amsterdam Cheese.* In case of emergency he never fails. Improves over time. In this WC he has demonstrated an extraordinary performance and leadership inside the field. He was the source of energy of the oranje midfield. Really good stick & body relation, he has shown some delicious skills. As a midfielder he combines the control of the game with some "rush" moments of acceleration. After two years of good maduration he will be in the best moment of his career in Tokyo.

Victor Wegnez: *Blitzkrieg Bop.* There is no WC championship without Wegnez and what he represents for Belgium. Belgium hockey needed his rock intervention and they will need him to continue winning. Accelerated drums and aggressive guitars but with a consistent bass. Victor is pure dynamite. Bright future ahead. He will have to learn how to play ballads as well, like Ramones eventually did, but without losing his true punk essence.

Blake Govers: *Uluru.* He is bigger than the rest. Imposing respect, admiration and fear to others. Blake is the offensive totem of Australia. He shines differently depending on the game. He can be good at progressing with the ball, he can be just a killer inside the circle or he can be a top drag flicker if needed. Blake is in the center of kookaburra's dreams. He will be essential in Tokyo.

Not a bad team, right?

EHL 18-19 Reflections

24/04/2019

The EHL is over and it's time to reflect about what we have seen these days in Eindhoven. I'm going to highlight 4 different factors:

The Format

This new EHL format, with the KO16, KO8 and FINAL4 all-in-one it's been really attractive for the spectators. In just one single event you had 6 days of top hockey. And during Easter, which is probably the best period to sit in the stands, with nice and smooth sunny days. However, for the players this tournament has been a physical torture. RWK and Polo had to play 4 top games in just 5 days. This is simply too much. WatDucks and Mannheim played the same 4 games but in 6 days. That extreme physical load would never take place in any other hockey event. And the consequences have been obvious: more injuries and a gradual decrease in the quality of the game played during the last stages of the tournament.

Shoot-outs

Out of 16 top games, 7 ended in SO's. And the 4 games of the KO8 were draws. For example, WatDucks, the champions, won the KO16, the KO8 and the semi-finals in the shootout tie-break! Watching the games I had the feeling that during the final stages of the games there was a tendency towards the draw (a kind of unconscious and invisible magnetic force). How many goals in the last 5' we have seen? How many epic comebacks? I'm sure there is a psychoanalytic underlying reason here.

Anyway, as coaches are we aware of the crucial importance of shootouts? How can we train them well? Do we have experts on that? Do we always train SO's with the same goalkeepers? How can we reproduce the same "pressure" context? How do we approach the shootout execution? With a predetermined plan? With a contingency plan? Or just improvisation? Do we give any instruction to our players? Or do they decide by themselves? And one more question: If SO's are so crucial, why not use the video-umpire in these "key" episodes? I don't understand it.

The Dutch-German Romance

The three dutch participants have been knocked out by german teams. Oranje-Rood lost against Mulheim. Amsterdam and Kampong lost against RWK. Only Amsterdam reached a draw after a 2-0 comeback in the last 10 minutes of the game. I will never say that "dutch" hockey is weaker than german hockey. Or that dutch teams have less mental strength than the germans. No, that would be too populist now. However, one thing is clear to me: most of the dutch teams put more attention in the attacking phase than in the defensive one. And they also put more attention in the offensive transition than in the defensive one. I have no doubt about it.

If you analyze the way in which dutch teams defend, everything is pretty standard. One team plays man to man, and another one plays zonal, but nothing really special. The function of the free-man is always stable and the pressure dynamics of the strikers are quite traditional and predictable. Now, if you can, take your time and analyze all the defensive variations that RWK showed in this EHL. And we find the same level of care/attention in the way they prepare the defensive transitions.

The problem of the vertical dutch game is also located immediately after losing the ball. The counter cover is not a vague principle that has to be reminded when we're attacking. No. The way we prepare our defensive transition must be in full coherence with the way we attack. If we constantly play line over lines and quick attacks, then we never can't have the team ready to put press after-loss. So we'll always have our defenders far from opposite strikers (Herzbruch) when we lose the ball. Taking this inherent limitation, are these dutch teams working hard on how to play a good back withdrawal? I don't think so. Energy, accelerations and give and go's, this is the dutch mantra.

Dutch teams, despite having great players, don't compete like Germans do. And I think that is because the "attention" given to the 4 phases of the game is not balanced. The game has 4 interrelated phases, and all must be well attended, prepared and practised.

Waterloo Ducks

The champions. Waterloo is famous for two things: the first one is because Waterloo is where our catalan president Puigdemont is exiled. The second one, and less important, is because of the battle that Napoleon lost in 1815. This belgian hockey team also played extremely good battles these days. And now Waterloo is also famous for this EHL. As I said earlier, the first three games were won in the SO's! The WatDucks were not in possession of the best attack of the tournament (although Ghislain is definitely someone to follow) but they had a very good and solid defensive unit with Van Strydonck, Boccard and Dohmen controlling the low central zone of the field, and specially Vincent Vanasch at the goal. The best goalkeeper of the world made the difference.

We don't have to reach big conclusions here. I think that Waducks won because Vanasch saved crucial goals in key moments, because they were comfortable and confident defending inside the circle and because they were lucky. I strongly believe that RWK and MHC are better teams than Waducks. And I believe that out of ten games, both Germans are able to win most of them. But that is bullshit and doesn't count. In this EHL, Waterloo Ducks have achieved an epic victory and they deserve the best credits for that.

God bless EHL!

UMPIRES AND OFFICIALS

Umpiring Field Hockey is essentially problematic

18/01/2018

Some weeks ago I had a discussion with Adrian Lock, the head coach of Spanish women's team. We were talking about how permissive we tend to be when we whistle our teams in training sessions. As coaches -and I'm sure this is a common attitude- we prefer to be permissive than too restrictive regarding the offenses we umpire.

Why? We know that if we don't blow the whistle, we will generate more transitions in the game, the more transitions we create, the more intensity we get, and more concentration and better physical requirement. Well, the question is: being much more permissive in training, are we creating more troubles, issues or conflicts than if we would umpire it with normal standards? No! Why? Then, what makes umpiring field hockey so problematic? Why do we constantly find critiques towards umpires (especially in domestic competitions)?

First of all, I decided to read the FIH Rules & Regulations trying to find the source of the problem. You don't have to be an expert in hermeneutics to find something intriguing: the concept "intention" and its variants appear 21 times within the text. This fact is meaningless until we compare it, for example, with Soccer Rules, where it appears 4 times. But not only "Intentionality", our text is also full of other problematic words like "unless", "danger", "gaining an advantage", "preventing", "probable", etc. What's wrong with these concepts? Relativity.

There are basically two types of actions that you can whistle, regarding its ontological nature: the facts and the interpretations. Judging the first one is easy. If the ball has touched the foot or not is a matter of fact. Same if the ball has crossed the line or not. Nowadays, and with the use of video umpire in international events, the only problem is to get the right perception/vision of the action. But why are interpretations so problematic? Because interpretations are subjective. If they are subjective, its validity comes from the subject. Was that contact too physical? Was that ball too dangerous? Was that tackle intentioned? Pure interpretation as you can see. And extra bonus: having 2 umpires at the same game, there are two different interpretations for the same event.

Of course, the subject-umpire follows a certain guideline that assesses his/her criteria: the Rules & Regulations Holy Bible. But the specific weight of interpretation in hockey is simply too heavy. That makes "umpiring well" an activity which is essentially impossible. Something unreachable.

And pragmatically, if you agree that umpiring well is impossible, umpiring becomes basically a way to impose the umpire's opinion above others (in order to preserve the order and not fall into chaos). Therefore, the abusement of power is the only natural behavior that we should expect from umpires. And the umpires, thrown to this "tyrannical" condition, fall in the temptation of repression through violence. The control of the game aims to be gained with too many interruptions, faults, cards and even propagandistic speeches.

My last point: if umpiring hockey is essentially problematic, due to its natural limitations, who is the good umpire? The one who gets peace without repression. When we (coaches) whistle, can we keep the game in peace without significant violence. Why? Because we have the respect from players. This respect is the basement of moral authority.

Get their respect without the whistle and they will respect your whistle forever.

No one else could have designed a sport worse than indoor hockey

05/02/2018

The indoor versions of outdoor sports are, by its a posteriori nature, born in a "slavery-state" that condemns its becoming. The only possible emancipation for these "indoorized" sports is the creation of a new identity, unattached from the old "master" and with its own personality, singularities, calendars, rules and different bodies of governance. Through the process of creation of this new identity/culture, it can happen that the new indoor sport denies the past submission (*aufhebung*) and starts creating its new history. We have seen this dialectical process in indoor football, for example. Nowadays nobody can state that indoor football is the "slave-version" of outdoor soccer, not even Hegel.

But In indoor hockey we're still in the master-slave primary step, where the fear of dying in indoor hockey represents its own condemnation and generates its own submission in front of the dominant power. Outdoor hockey enjoys this condition. In our case, this slavery status is even more perverted, because it's been designed from the origin. It's formed in its DNA because indoor has been designed by outdoor hockey as a contingency plan during winter stops. Indoor hockey never had real autonomy.

Now let's focus on the visible aspects of indoor hockey misfortune. Let's analyze why indoor hockey is ugly, cripple and will never be successful in the current context. Warning here: when you find a sport which is only loved by some experts (first, I wrote "nerds"), you have a suspicious signal that something is wrong.

Do an experiment: bring a common sports person into an indoor hall and try to explain to him/her how indoor hockey works. Try to explain why the ball can't be controlled in the air; or why the ball can't be played against the blocks of the defenders; or why the players can't touch each other because it's "physical game offense"; or why the players can't play from the floor cause only 3 contact points are allowed; or why the players cannot hit the ball with certain techniques; or why after a free hit...no, don't even try to explain that.

The only "spectacular" moment that we have in indoor hockey is the penalty corner, and it is spectacular because of the extreme risk that it represents for the defenders. The roman circus was spectacular for the pleb too. I think that we should get rid of penalty corners as soon as possible.

In Germany they love indoor hockey because they have invented it, they rule the sport in their manner (let's play 30' per half guys), they have a long season so they have enough time to take it seriously.

Trying to constructive and thinking about a new variant of indoor hockey that can be nice and funny, here there are 6 new proposals from my side:

1. The ball can be played in the air like in outdoor hockey. Players would stop defending with the stick down, like it has happened in the outdoor version. Therefore new passing lines will be opened and more elimination dribblings will be seen.

2. A bit lighter and bigger ball. So less danger for its impact (no more anti-blocking faults) and quicker and better ball for 3D skills.

3. New sticks with bigger heads and wider bodies. Better for 3D controls.

4. Smaller GK kids. Better agility of the goalkeepers and nice saves.

5. Shootout instead of a penalty corner. Its conversion rate is similar and is not dangerous at all.

6. The physical contact is allowed like it is allowed in basketball or indoor football. Higher degree of tolerance towards it (shoulders contact is allowed, for example)

Briefly, indoor hockey should aim to be completely different and more attractive to common people. Indoor should develop its own identity and perhaps that means to have an independent body of governance and parallel calendars. To assume duplicity. In terms of rules and equipment I think that there is still a lot to do in order to make it more spectacular and less weird. Here I just gave some "provocative proposals" but this topic should be broadly and deeply addressed.

I love indoor hockey. But I love it due to my vice, not its virtue.

The Indoor Hockey Frustration

16/01/2019

Last weekend we had the indoor finals of the Catalan Cup. This season the Catalan Hockey Federation tried to give more "credit" to indoor hockey while organizing a 3-weekend competition with 8 teams. In women we only had 4 teams participating. Last year our indoor season in Catalonia took place in just 1 weekend. Yes, 1 weekend. Here there are some of my reflections after the finals.

I'm not a big fan of the way indoor hockey is managed today. In my opinion there are some rules that are truly counter-intuitive and generate surreal game situations. For example, when many players are standing at the corner and nobody can do anything. Ridiculous. Also this rule "ball against the block" is also something that creates lots of troubles because it's purely based on subjective interpretation if it was "deliberate" or not. And this is essentially problematic. This is what we have: acceptance.

In Mens, Atlètic Terrassa won the final against Club Egara. The result of the game was 3-2. Umpires showed 12 cards in total. Yes, I repeat: a dozen.

Since indoor hockey started to be discriminated against and underestimated by our local hockey institutions (clubs and federations), the level of the game in Catalonia has gradually and continuously decreased. Atlètic Terrassa, the champion, has been combining indoor and outdoor training during these 3 indoor weeks. In total they have trained 4 indoor sessions. Another critical factor against the level of indoor is that the best teams from Catalonia don't want to play the Nationals because they don't want to lose weeks from the outdoor preparation. Coaches believe that participating in indoor competitions has less impact than outdoor training sessions. This is the current belief among catalan coaches.

We have a sport that is different from its outdoor version, with many different rules that makes the game very demanding and singular. Quick decision-making, first touch combinations, particular set pieces, etc. While field hockey is a pure non-linear game, indoor is different. In indoor hockey you can apply more mechanisms, establish fixed positions and prepare plans. The environment is more closed, let's say.

On the one hand we have this demanding sport and on the other we have teams that are not investing enough time and preparation for it. What is the result? The outcome is obvious: the level of the game diminishes. We have outdoor players inside the indoor court. 15 years ago the level in Spain was much higher than now, with our National Team competing in the A division of the European Cup Nations and spanish clubs achieving medals in European Cups.

This current lack of quality in indoor hockey creates frustration. We see players in ball possession without any idea of what to do. The pressure from the environment brings them to put the head down, dribble or play blind balls. Dribbling generates more chaotic transitions and playing blind balls result in attacking offenses. More frustration.

If players get frustrated because they can't cope with the high demands of the sport, coaches get frustrated too. They want to play good indoor hockey but the players are not prepared for that. If players and coaches get frustrated, umpires too. When the game becomes chaotic and over-emotional, and considering that indoor is difficult to umpire *per se*, now imagine if it's played by frustrated players and coaches. Our umpires are not used to umpire many "top" indoor games due to our micro-seasons, so they don't have the proper expertise.

But that's not all. Spectators also become frustrated. They feel the chaotic and libidinous nature of the event that is taking place. Spectators don't fully understand the rules, they don't know the complexity of the tactics and the difficulty of skills either. But they know that yelling to umpires can be beneficial. So they scream like mammals in heat. And that is a vicious circle, when the crowd starts screaming, players become more anxious so their decision-making impoverishes, the game becomes more chaotic, more chaos frustrates coaches and spectators. And again and again. 12 cards in the final. 12 cards in a single match.

This is a story of decadence. Indoor hockey is really important for our kids in Spain. Seasons of U14, U16 and U18's are, at least, 6-8 weeks long. The kids know how to play, they have enough time to practise and they improve a lot during the season. But when they make the final step to seniors everything fades away. Indoor hockey is beheaded in Spain.

Spanish Federation wants to recuperate the indoor national team again. That's very good news after the great disaster that was its past dissolution. How to "empower" indoor hockey again? Extending the season as-much-as-we-can could help. Clubs: sign your teams to indoor. Coaches: train as much as you can, train mechanisms, tactical variations and create pressure environments. Players: watch some videos from the german league and try to copy some of their skills, because they're the best in the world. Spectators: read Daniel Goleman or stay home. If we do that, the umpires will naturally improve with us and things will get better and better. The indoor hockey cycle can be virtuous again but we have to change the current dynamic immediately.

If indoor hockey is played well, indoor hockey is refined and delicious. But if indoor hockey is played bad, indoor hockey really sucks. So let's revive it or kill it, but see it dying is not funny anymore.

Philosophy & Video Umpires

29/10/2019

Hockey world has been blushed by the video umpire (VU) episode of the 2nd game between Canada and Ireland (Olympic Men Qualifier). Former players, coaches, umpires and social network agents have been extensively discussing "the action" and its dramatic consequences: discussing if it was deliberate or not, if the player contacted the leg or not, etc. Here I just wanted to bring some different ideas into the discussion, some reflections inspired by some philosophical masters.

Michel Foucault

"There are no facts, only interpretations." This philosophical quote is famously attributed to Friedrich Nietszche. Foucault took the argument and brought it further. He stated that "the power creates

the truth". Given a single fact every individual creates its own truth. However, it's the power, the agent who dominates the means, the one that produces and imposes a single truth over the other.

Hockey is a sport that is impossible to whistle well. The rules and regulations are full of interpretations and are too reliant on subjectivity. It is the power (the umpires) the agent that imposes the truth over the players. It is very easy to blame the umpire when they say "ball touched the foot" and the ball never touched it. However, things become more difficult when umpires judge intentions, danger, enough contact to fall, etc. Things become ugly.

If umpiring well is impossible, the feeling of "injustice", soon or late, arrives to everyone. Not because the VU was right or wrong but because the VU imposes a truth which is not necessarily shared by another subject. But that happens in every game.

Just for your information: in football, when the advice from the Video Umpire is about a "subjective" decision, the main umpire must "review" the image on the field and take the final decision by him/herself. In hockey, due to our different system, the last call belongs to the VU and the field umpire must obey.

Jürgen Habermas

The german philosopher spoke about "discursive ethics" and the enormous value of dialogue and consensus. For Habermas, every consistent argument is suitable to be discussed and it's precisely through discussion how we are able to achieve common agreements. So, why don't we have 2 video umpires? If we had two video umpires instead of just one, they could discuss every subjective interpretation, right? And why is there no discussion between VU and field umpires? Do we need this "imposition of truth" from only one omniscient umpire?

Assuming that there is no truth, the best solution for Habermans would have been an open dialogue between umpires, where they share interpretations of what they have seen, intentions and they finally agree in a form of consensus.

Byung Chul-Han

The korean philosopher wrote about the "transparency society". For him, we live in a "positive" society that doesn't accept any kind of negativity or resistance. No dissention or conflict. Everything must be flat and transparent. We tend to believe that transparency brings confidence, but that is the big fallacy. It is precisely in societies where there is no trust, when transparency emerges as a need. With trust, there is no need to see and check every process from inside. Life should be sensual, not pornographic.

Our video umpiring system is pornographic. We have a camera inside the cabin and we can hear every word from the umpires, every conversation. The digital panopticon is here. Big Brother. Umpires are aware that thousands of anonymous spectators are present, standing next to them in the crucial moment of taking the decision. I don't want to see and hear the video umpire! Let them talk openly among them but secretly for us! Let them discuss, show weakness, let them say "I don't know" or "it's complicated" or "what if". If we trust them, let them remain occult. It is because we don't trust them that we made them transparent. For your information, in football you can't hear the discussions from the umpires.

Dear umpires: your job is difficult and essentially problematic. You should have the right to discuss with your colleagues without the surveillance of the others. You might believe that transparency is good for the show and you might feel cool when others are watching you. You like to be exposed, as everyone else. But that's not real. You should have your own privacy. Your conversations must be "yours", not "ours", and there must be a private space where you can show your humanity, doubts, fears and dissensions.

You are the ones that will sentence us. So please, do it well.

CLUBS AND MANAGERS

Terrassa: The Hockey Talent Factory

27/02/2018

Terrassa is probably one of the most important hockey towns in the world. Within our 250.000 population city, we have 1 olympian player for every 2.000 citizens. And we just have 5 hockey clubs (being Atlètic Terrassa, Club Egara, and CD Terrassa, its big representatives). However, we've been producing some of the best hockey athletes in the world for decades. Ventalló, Colomer, Comerma, Dinarès, Amat, Escudé, Sala, Malgosa, Freixa, Alegre, Oliva...are some of the most iconic hockey surnames from Terrassa. The case of RC Polo and Júnior FC is quite similar as well, but they're more isolated in other cities. In Catalonia hockey is quite a "ghetto" sport, located in very few places but with super high returns in performance. No doubt that it's all about quality instead of quantity.

Everything started with a cultural exchange between industrial English and Catalan families. The English were living or often visiting Catalonia for business purposes (textile industry). This foreign community got in contact with our local rich families, most of them owners of capital. Some of these catalan families decided to send their sons to the UK in order to adopt new textile skills. Some of them came back from these exchanges with hockey sticks inside their bags. Hockey became part of that cultural-merchant exchange. A leisure activity for the industrial bourgeois. RCPolo of Barcelona adopted the sport and at the same time hockey got established at Terrassa, a growing textile town.

Roughly that was the origin. Given that background, the question that arises is: how that exclusive and elitist context achieved great hockey performance in the following decades? Let's talk about talent, youth development and performance. And let's mix these ideas with concepts like identity, social recognition and power.

First of all we need to understand how talent is converted into performance. We have many studies, models, academics and theories about that. There is no magic equation. But researchers like Jean Côté have collected significant data that may help us to understand the concept of talent development in youth ages. Here there are some conclusions and postulates derived from his investigations, and how they're represented in Terrassa:

Small-cities provide a better environment for youth sports development. To have a smaller environment brings more safety and control to the children. In Terrassa, we have most of our hockey community living in the center of the city (more expensive area). Kids go to very few schools in the center. They walk home and everything is well settled. Short distances from home to school and from school to the club.

Stronger supportive relationships. Integration. It's common to have former hockey players in families. Friends from school and friends from hockey are similar groups. Teachers are also familiar with hockey and they support the students when conflicts between studies and hockey emerge. Hockey trainers and coaches are well known for families. Everything is linked and interrelated. A bit endogamic.

A sense of belonging. When there is a social group well defined that automatically creates a sense of belonging. "We" are not "them". That brings social recognition and self-esteem in return. That is a source of positive social norms. It shapes singular habits and behaviors. The Terrassa hockey community has its own personality, social conducts, and even its own slang.

Contact with role-models. Every community has role-models. Personalities that represent and exemplify the higher aims of the participants. In our Terrassa hockey community, these role models are really close to the children. The ones that are not directly family-related, are youth coaches or friends from relatives. The kids can easily interact with their idols. This position is a source of motivation and passion. The idol is at the right aspirational distance. Not too close, not too far.

Tradition facilitates deliberate-play and the consequent specialization. LTAD Model (Long Term Athlete Development) states that in early ages the deliberate play (playing for fun) is fundamental. Not deliberate practice! When hockey is forged into our community DNA (the first gift after a birth is a hockey stick), to play hockey for fun becomes natural. For example: when we were kids together with Santi Freixa we spent hours playing hockey at the club. Playing without any "adult-made" guidance, being far from our parents and without any pressure or expectation. Another example: Teun de Nooijer started hockey when he was 9 years-old and just for fun. He never trained more than 2 days per week until he was 16 years-old. And he never hired any "personal coach", of course. However, he was sleeping next to his hockey stick. That is the point: to love the sport. The more fun kids can get, the more intrinsic motivation they will gain. As hockey clubs, can we promote more deliberate play? Yes, we can. How? While promoting social engagement and designing deliberate-play opportunities. We should create hockey apostles, not hockey slaves.

High-Performance Programs. After the first stages when kids become adolescents it's time to invest more time in the regular practice of the sport. Now it's the moment of deliberate-practice. More hours or practise. Train to train and train to compete, according to LTAD. With the passion for hockey previously adopted and good values integrated, the teenager is now ready to approach the sport from a different point of view. Other hockey peers will bring new social recognition beyond family. To perform well in hockey becomes an important indicator for this social recognition. The kid is ready to gradually convert the passion for hockey into a high-performance mentality. Now there is a clear goal and a purpose. To be part of the Catalan U15's is probably one of the first "performance" targets that motivate our local kids. And frustration arises too. These highly engaged players will accept and demand more hours of training. If clubs are able to get good hockey coaches and prepare wise programs, players will make a huge technical growth from 13 to 18 years old. But be careful, If during the childhood parents have deposited too many expectations onto the kid, during the adolescence the kid will reject the sport as part of the negation of parental authority. I've seen so many hockey talented players wasting their potential top-sport career due to external pressures from parents.

Terrassa is not a miracle. Its success as "Hockey Town" has some key factors, as I tried to explain. Terrassa possesses a particular socio cultural environment (still bourgeois) that constantly generates talent. And Terrassa also has good hockey clubs with professional structures that are able to convert this raw talent into great performance. However there is still work to do. These days we're facing important troubles like parental early-performance-selection demands. We have budget constraints that restrict our capacity to hire top coaches in youth ages. And also we suffer space capacity constraints that limitate the number of hours that we can invest in youth athletes. We're training less than what we should train.

Competitive forces have increased. Other good hockey programs are settled in Barcelona, Madrid and other parts of Spain. The capital tends to concentrate the best resources around, and if Terrassa wants to maintain its privileged position in the near future, it would need something else besides our romantic hockey story. We will have to invest in smart development projects, good professionals, and top teams.

The Golden Squad

23/03/2018

Every player is different and every squad is unique. However as coaches or managers we should try to reduce this complexity into something measurable. This is the only way we can manage our players according to some principles, constants, and indicators. And when we are talking about squad management (the selection criteria), we should take some of these guidelines into account. This text is just an invitation for a reflection and self-analysis, for clubs, coaches or just for hockey fans.

Some time ago, during a club meeting about our hockey ladies-side project, our general director came up with the following contribution: let's distribute our hockey players in three different groups: Talent players (Tt's), Top players (Tp's) and Club players (Cb's). First of all, let's see the main characteristics of these three categories:

Talent Players (Tt's): These guys are young, they still don't have a broad experience, just talent. They have been involved in youth regional & national programs and nowadays they're playing for the U18 or U21 of the country. They are players with chances to reach the national team in the near future. On the pitch, they're still not regular in their performance. What do they need? To gain experience as soon as possible. Intense training in decision-making under pressure and the integration of tactical concepts. They must be completed technically. We should assign them responsibilities, give them minutes at the top level and let them fail repeatedly. They must invest in hockey with full determination. Your Tp's represent their role models and the Cb's will show them the intrinsic values of the team.

Top Players (Tp's): The best players in your squad. They are in the orbit of the national team, either in the current selection or close to be selected. Sunday by Sunday they perform above 8 and make differences. They are physically top athletes and technical genius with the stick. What do they need? To have the proper environment and resources to perform at their best level. They require autonomy from the coach and enough room for creativity. They deserve a unique treatment. Make them supportive with others and not selfish. They must be tough with the Tt's and respectful with the Cp's.

Club Players (Cb's): Either former international players in their last career stage or others that never made it. They're above 23 and have already played a good number of domestic seasons. They've shared a squad with many different mates and also some different coaches. Lots of experiences loved. They are consistent and perform a 6 or 7 every game. They really know about team culture and values. These players are not the fittest ones, nor the most skillful anymore. But knowing their limitations, they can perform well because they are intelligent. What do they need? We should define very clear roles for them, so they know what we expect from them. They are crucial in any team process because they are the "social glue" that you always need. Give them confidence and engage them as "educators" of the team. If they're not happy and motivated you cannot build any successful team in the long-run. They should protect the Tt's and keep Tp's on track if needed.

Given these three categories, the second thing we can do is to analyze some top teams from Europe and check what compositions they have, according to our model. What proportions of these 3 categories do they have in their squads? Well, I'll save you some precious time now. After analyzing 15 top clubs (men) from Europe (Germany, Holland, Belgium and Spain) I've found that the average proportion of these squads (aka the "golden ratio squad"), is:

The Golden Squad: 33% Tt's + 33% Tp's + 33% Cb's

In other words, do you want to set up a successful team? Get 6 internationals, 6 U21/U18's and 6 senior experienced players. And then start to work!

Every team has its singularity. For example, we have teams specialized in Tp's, like Bloemendaal or Rot-Weiss Köln, with many "stars" in the squad. There are other clubs where besides top's they also provide chances to many talented players. Teams like RCPolo, Dragons, Kampong or Rotterdam HC. And finally, we have other teams where most of their selection is based on Cb's players. Curiously this is quite common in Spain, with Atlètic Terrassa and Club Egara as good representatives but especially Júnior FC.

The last question can be: how can we shape these players? Well, the ideal pathway is the one where our youth players become talent players. For this initial stage, you need to have good "talent boost" programmes at your club as well as good technical coaches in your U16 and U18 teams. Once you're able to produce talent you should turn them into top's. For this crucial stage you need a good head coach with the special ability to "develop" players. And once top players decide to step back from the international level you should try to retain them as club players, so they can deliver to others the experience that they previously gained. However, this utopian flow is not always the case.

On the contrary, the system collapses when we are not able to turn our youngsters into talent's, our talent's into top's and our top's into club's. Then we find counter-intuitive cases like youngsters becoming club players when they're just 21 or 22. And that's the case to avoid.

As coaches, are we taking this "golden rule" into account when we design our squad? Are we treating our players according to what they need? As clubs, do we strategically decide what category are we going to expand or reduce? If so, do we know how to do it?

Assuming the scarcity as a premise, where do we allocate our limited resources? Where do we invest our time and energy?

12 Tips from Antoine-Henri Jomini on Making a Perfect Team

23/10/2018

This article is about a famous master in the art of war: Antoine-Henri Jomini (1779-1869). In this book you find another text based on another war master: Carl von Clausewitz. Both characters are coetaneous, but there is no evidence of meeting between them. If Clausewitz was more a philosopher of the war, Jomini was more an engineer of it. Now let's see what Jomini can teach us.

Jomini was a swiss talented general wisely recruited by the french army under Napoleon. Later on, he was seduced by the Russians and was flirting with both armies for some years. Pure swiss neutrality. He ended his days living in Brussels and writing manuals about military strategy and tactics. His most famous work is "The Art of War" (1838). The book is a huge theoretical compendium about war and the text is still used as a reference guide at the West Point Academy in the US.

After reading the book I've decided to select a particular fragment where Jomini numbers the 12 essential conditions in making a perfect army (chapter 2, article XIII). Let's see how these 12 ingredients also can apply into our sport and the way we design our own squads.

To Have a Good Recruiting-System: The selection of our players is important. We need to determine our criteria. When we recruit, are we considering the positions of the players and our vacancies? Or do we do it regarding their skills? Is there any particular preferred "style of play" that we are looking for? When recruiting are we trying to fulfill our game model? Or we select players and then, according to them, we design the game model? When and how are we approaching new players? Do we have a good network of contacts overseas? Who and how do we try to seduce them?

A Good Organization: Try to make sure that your team is well organized. By well organized I mean clarity in roles and clarity in the way that conflicts should be managed and solved within the team. Everybody should know how to proceed in case of incidence. Decisions must be taken following criterias previously explained to everyone and accepted by all parties.

A Well-Organized System of National Reserves: In our sport that means to have a good system of youth and talent development. Importing talent is always more expensive and less effective than producing it. But to manufacture talent requires more time and patience. It is crucial to invest time and resources into our "reserves". Do we have a proper career plan for our players in the youth ages? Do we have any kind of "talent boost" program in our club? Are we working in coherence with our junior team? And do we have any kind of development squad?

Good instruction of officers and men in drill and internal duties as well as those of a campaign: Instruction means Training. Our team must be well trained. A good training program comprises skills, principles and match structures/mechanisms. We must design, combine and periodize all of these elements and make sure that our players assimilate them. Here it is important to have a good staff besides you, to have people that can be fully responsible and become experts in different training tasks (physical trainer, skills coach, drill design, trainer, attack/defense coach, IT, PC specialist, etc).

A strict but not humiliating discipline, and a spirit of subordination and punctuality, based on conviction rather than on formalities of the service: This point is about the capacity from our members to fit and work into a bigger organization. Sometimes the final decisions adopted in the team are not aligned with yours. We should set up a state of obedience without the use of force or repression. For that purpose we need good discursive tools as well as a charismatic leadership.

A well-digestive system of rewards, suitable to excite emulation: If Clausewitz talked about honour and renown, now Jomini talks about rewards. And I repeat: we should provide social recognition to our players. That can be organized using a system that rewards factors like behaviours, performance or experience. This system of rewards can be purely subjective or can be based on different KPIs. The aim is the same at the end: to have our players motivated and to set up role models for the rest (to set an example of how everybody should behave).

The special arms of engineering and artillery to be well instructed: Beyond the education of our troops we should take care of our special weapons. In our case that means set-pieces. Do we have a wide range of offensive PC variations? Are we able to play different PC defenses? Do we have any special plan for long corners and free-hits? These "closed" situations, if properly trained, can have big returns in your performance.

An armament superior, if possible, to that of the enemy, both as to defensive and offensive arms: If possible, try to sign the best players as you can. Best players will be the source of your offensive and defensive power. By best players I mean best performances. When your armament is superior is when you can effectively cause more damage to your opponent. It's about recruiting, of course, but is also about the capacity that we can have as coaches to make our players better than the rest.

A general staff capable of applying these elements, and having an organization calculated to advance the theoretical and practical education of its officers: The development of our staff is a crucial factor for Jomini. We should have an organization that takes care of our staff, their interests and their careers. Are we organizing enough coaching courses for our young trainers and coaches? Do we have a structure that promotes and enhances its development? Are the different teams and staffs well interrelated between each other? Does knowledge flow well across the network of coaches?

A good system for the commissariat, hospitals, and of general administration: You can have good players and top coaches, but you need good complementary professionals around too. In our sport case, that means to have a good team manager, nutritionist, analyst, psychologist, doctor and every other expert that can bring an extra value into the team process.

A good system of assignment to command, and of directing the principle operations of war: Try to make sure that the club or the national association where you are working is well structured. Structured in different levels of responsibility and structured in different fields of knowledge. A good structure also means an organization with shared values, a common mission and vision. And these three strategic elements must be well embodied (expressed and represented) across the whole organization.

Exciting and keeping alive the military spirit of the people: To keep alive the military spirit of the people = to keep alive the competitive spirit of our players. Try to excite them in the joy of competing. In the pleasure of growing through victory and defeat. In the long run you will only prevail if the spirit of competing is well integrated into your players. Very important: it's not about enjoying victories, it's about loving the game.

I'll will finish with a quote of "The Wisdom of the Sands" that just came into my mind:

> *"Constrain them to join in building a tower, and you shall make them like brothers. But if you would have them hate each other, throw food amongst them." Antoine de Saint-Exupéry*

How to waste your Talented Players

06/11/2018

As I explained in my text "Terrassa, the hockey talent factory" there are various key elements that jointly produce a huge amount of talent in Terrassa (Spain). Today we're going to address the management and the challenges that we face as a club once this talent is produced.

If we're talking about talent creation in Terrassa, we all think about players like Amat, Tubau, Freixa, Bonastre, Alegre, Oliva, Enrique, Lleonart and many others. Terrassa is proud of these players, guys that were borned here have achieved the top international level. But this article is not dedicated to them. This article is dedicated to another set of talents. Players that once were labeled as "precious pearls" but they never made the last step to the top level. Players that somehow were lost in translation. Does it sound familiar? Well, let's start. If we talk about talent management, we can differentiate 4 different stages:

Incubation: The way we think about talent is linear. Cause and effect. We consider talent as a badge of qualities that everyone is able to acquire if there is enough time, energy and work invested. The underlying paradigm that sustains this belief is the old industrial paradigm (the same that still guides most of our educational programs). So the more that we invest in youth ages the better performance we will achieve. This is a fallacy. The only thing that as a club we can do in early ages is to design the proper context where talent can flourish. Nothing else.

Detection: During adolescence is when we could start detecting talent. Not earlier. I repeat, not earlier. How do we make these detection? Well, basically taking two factors into consideration: the motor skills (movement) and the decision-making (criterion).

Development: Once we detect some talents in our hockey institution, then we should create a special boost program for them. From 13-14 to 17-18 years old approximately. It's time to shape this gross talent into something nice, like artisans do. Our hockey institution should support our talents in 4 different areas: Skills Development, Tactical Principles, Mental Coaching and Environmental Support.

Performance: The last step of the process is when our talent reaches the top level competition and is able to perform well on a regular basis. So consistency in performance must be the main quality to achieve at this stage. Ups and downs are typically in talents, but not in great performers. When a regular performance is achieved our talent is not only in possession of an extraordinary set of skills and a good game sense. Now our player is also in possession of mental strength, social intelligence and working culture. We have a top athlete.

That was just my proposal about how talent can be managed within our clubs and federations. A proper management will create a context where this talent can be well incubated, detected, developed and finally converted into top performance. However, although we commonly have good structures, we all have seen lots of cases where young talents failed in becoming top athletes. And I think that we never have dedicated enough attention to these "dark" cases. Now is time to highlight these stories.

The sooner that we get results the better. The sooner that we start investing the bigger returns we will get. And what it works for start-up companies also works for kids. We as adults tend to interpret childhood as a means, never as an end in itself. We're living in a society that is pathologically addicted to performance. Everything is measured according to its results. That is the reason why we don't play anymore, now we only compete. And that is a huge difference.

This ideology shapes and constitutes everything we see and we do around the hockey field. And when we educate our kids we project the same underlying premises. We demand high academic ranks, and if they are not achieved then we pay academies. In hockey, from a very young age, our federations organize competitions where the pools are distributed according to the level of the kids. And these league systems are based on competition: matches, scores and tables. Therefore, as soon as we detect a kid that is more capable than others (runs quicker, reacts faster or is just taller) we put our "adult focus" there. When they are very young these kids start playing for the "first team" of their age group, and this team becomes the "crown jewel" of the club. The place to be.

Parents feel super proud of having their kid at the top of the tier. It represents a kind of symbolic reward for the good educational work that they did during childhood. And this social reward is addictive. All very unconscious, don't blame them yet. Parents, again applying the capitalist logic, understand that other competitive forces can change the *status quo*, so they push the kid to perform better in order to maintain this high-cast privilege that makes them happy. So we find parents attending training sessions, recording matches, giving coaching talks, paying for personal trainers and sending the kid to different hockey camps all over the continent. And the funny thing is that if you ask them they always say: we do that "because this is what my kid wants". Holy ignorance. The desire of the child is always to fulfill the expectation of the parent.

Then the kid reaches the crucial stage of adolescence. Adolescence is characterized by the impulse of rebellion against parental authority. The negation of the boss. The child rejects every aspect from parents, including their hockey projections of course. And at this stage when we find teenagers trying to "escape" from parental influence through various means.

We find many wasted talents at this stage. In most of the cases the primary reason is the high level of expectations deployed on them. In adolescence we find players quitting from hockey, others continue playing but struggling because they have developed some "bad boy" behaviours. These hiper-frustrated players face difficulties in tolerating any trace of error. And remember, frustration is always directly proportional to expectations. During their childhood these "talented players" have been treated differently. Now, when they have to work hard like everyone else, they can't do it well. When these players finally reach the first senior team they are not "the one" anymore. Now they share a team with other top players as well. Our talented players feel frustration because things are more difficult. Now they don't score as many times as they were doing. Now they lose more balls because opponents are better. Now they miss and fail repeatedly, and they were not trained for this particular battlefield. They are not ready to confront this new reality.

What do we do as coaches? because we find a player that is so talented, someone who has always been the best of the generation, but now this player is struggling and underperforming. We have two options: either we face the problem and we try to "re-educate" the player under this new context, or we deny the problem and remove the player from the squad. The second is the easiest one. The first one requires time, energy and brings more troubles.

These guys think that they deserve everything but they are not willing to pay the price that everything costs. There are the first ones in demand, but the last ones in delivering. And they try to hide their unconscious frustration with excuses like "this is not fair". Victimism beats responsibility.

But coach, it was our responsibility as educators to support these players across that long development process and obviously we didn't do it well. It's not their failure, it's ours. And now it's too late. They have become a new "wasted talent" in this dark list. A list that no one is proud of. So this article is dedicated to all of them. Eternal promising players that never made it.

Never give up with a talented player. The challenge is worth it.

Firenze Talent Club

21/04/2020

Firenze (Florence) is considered the capital of the Renaissance (15th and 16th centuries approximately). The renaissance is the golden stage of history that links the middle age with modernity. After a long and dark middle age decadence, after the disastrous Black Death and after the fall of Constantinople, the ancient tradition from Greece and Rome was revived in western Europe. That return to the "humanitas" specially took place in Firenze and in other city-states of taly. Some rich families of bankers like the Medicici, and due to the previous invention of the double-entry accountancy, took the power -see Machiavelli- and decided to start "sponsoring" artists. Why did they decide that? Well, don't be naive here: good reputation in front of the citizens and moral atonement in front of God (nice partnerships with the Pope by the way).

So we can state that without this patronage, it would have been very difficult for artists to flourish. Resources are still essential today if we pretend to transform raw talent into great performers.

Brunelleschi, Da Vinci, Raffaello, Boticelli, Michelangelo, etc were all "supported" by the Medicis.

Now let's focus on how this art was practically developed. Most of these artists organized themselves through workshops *(Bottegas)*. These workshops were well structured organizations. Don't imagine something bohemian where some artists are just freely creating in a co-working freelance environment. Not at all! Those workshops were more similar to a current company, where "productivity" was an important KPI. The Master was at the top of the pyramid, and under him there were officials and then apprentices at the bottom. Some of the "bottegas" were multidisciplinary, so "artists" were having a broad education far from restrictive specialization. The most famous example here is the workshop of Verrochio, from where Da Vinci emerged as sculptor, painter and even architect. That approach is also something that we should consider when we talk about talent development.

The process of educating the apprentices and the officials were through specificity, that is, while working. That's very important. There were no manuals, books or formal academies where you could learn a theoretical corpus of knowledge. The talent development was based on the artistic creation: gestures, movements, the boost of intuition, perception and sensibility. This "learning by doing" and the presence of direct feedback from the Master in situ was proven to be the most effective way to develop the artists, and that is also the most effective way to develop our players today.

Apprentices were joining the workshops at the age of 12 approximately. Both parties, the Master and the apprentice family had to sign contracts where the Master explained all the learning outcomes that the apprentices would achieve but also what were his obligations in front of them: the Master took care of the education but also about the supply of clothes, food and sometimes even a form of remuneration. This is also relevant: the education was not only related to the activity as such, but also included and covered other live factors / needs of the apprentice. If we bring this into our daily context, clubs should also take care of other aspects in the life of our players (studies, family, wellbeing, etc). Game performance is a complex phenomenon.

The role of the Master was also significant for the apprentice talent development in the sense that it was common for apprentices to practise their technique while copying existing artworks from the Master. Therefore, the way the apprentice was shaped was influenced by the Master, who was the first role model that they had. However, when officials were able to become Masters of their own workshops, they were taking new stylistic pathways and techniques. It is very important for our talents to have clear role models from where they can take references from. These role models can be coaches and/or other team mates.

The last lesson I would like to highlight from the florece workshops is the indivisibility between science and art. Today we're quite often making this division between both bodies, but during the renaissance both things were coexisting harmoniously. For example, it was due to the linear perspective that architects became more productive and effective in the design of their buildings. Or remember the famous "Vitriuvius Man" of Da Vinci, where mathematical proportions and the concept of beauty were directly linked. There is no artist without technique and knowledge, but the acquisition of this "scientific" knowledge doesn't make the art to automatically appear. In our case, for player development we have the same combination: they require intelligent plans based on scientific evidence (training methodologies, physical conditioning, data analysis…). However, that is just a necessary condition, but not sufficient, for the great talent to emerge.

Briefly, what can we learn from the workshops of the renaissance?

- Talent Development requires resources and vision.

- The organization of the educational pathway is essential. But this organization should not be restrictive for the players. It should enable as many capacities as possible.

- The most effective way to boost the talent is from the specificity, that is, while playing under coaching guidelines.

- Talent players require support in all dimensions, not only in the performance of the game.

- Players need role models from where they can get ideas, behaviours and values.

- Coaching talented players is a mixture of science and art, we need to cultivate the sensibility and intuition but at the same time we require the best proven practises and scientific findings.

Talent needs to be sculpted. Make sure you have the proper marble, scarp and master.

COACHES

Deconstructing Game Mechanisms

04/10/2020

The present text emerges with the objective to bring some light to the famous dialectic between game mechanisms and principles. These two concepts: mechanisms and principles, often have been taken as antagonists and we had high-performance coaches who were advocating for more mechanisms and other coaches who were in favour of less mechanisms and more principles. Well, first of all let's see what is the meaning of these two concepts and then we will explain how we can dissolve this apparent controversy.

When I say "mechanisms" I mean the predetermined patterns of movement that we as coaches teach to our players to do inside the field. It's about providing a set of instructions that must be taken given a particular context. Actually, it's not about deciding but about executing or obeying. For example, we tell our left defender that every ball she receives, she should play along the line if possible. Or we can tell our midfielders to overload the right-hand side of the field every time we build-up from the back.

Mechanisms are movements that can easily be drawn on a whiteboard and can easily be clicked in our game analysis software. What most of the coaches do when they analyse a hockey game is precisely to detect patterns of movement (to detect mechanisms) and, later on, prepare counter measures (other mechanisms) to beat them. It's like a chess battle.

Mechanisms, structure, discourse, modelling the reality. The more resources we spend in "automatizing" our game, the more mechanisms we will define and provide to our players. The total set of mechanisms that we establish is the way we play, according to some coaches.

But we have principles as well. Principles are guidelines that orientate our decision-making process. It's less aggressive. It brings more autonomy to the subject, more freedom. A principle is an interpretative tool that once applied in a particular context provides meaning and orientates the response. You can't draw a principle on a whiteboard, or more precisely, you can draw it in many places. You can click principles on a video but a priori you don't know exactly where and when you'll find them. If we can compare mechanisms with syntaxis, we can relate principles to semantics.

For example, "Draw and Pass" is a principle. The player will match any particular situation with this principle and will take the proper decision. "Face the Play", "Stick to Stick", "Hit & Hope", "Give & Go", "Line over Line" or "Guard" can be other principles that we normally use in our teams. None of these principles tells you who, where, when and how you will do it.

So the question that arises is: what should we do as coaches? Should we create our game style based on predetermined mechanisms? Or should we put the focus on building up principles? Well, the solution is the synthesis of both. And we will reach that synthesis while using deconstruction.

"Deconstruction" is a philosophical concept that comes from Heidegger, but Jacques Derrida was the one who made it famous. Don't try to read these two guys unless you want to solve your insomnia without drugs. Briefly and roughly, "deconstruction" is the art of dismantling structures. Deconstruction is the process of analyzing the underlying structures of any discourse with the aim of discovering something fundamental that is not obvious. So deconstruction has a creative factor, it is not a fixed method or technique.

In my opinion, what coaches should do when taking over a team is to deconstruct the current style of play of that team. Teams are never a *tabula rasa* (blank slate), and this is the first mistake we can do: try to build-up something ignoring what is already built there previously. In this process of deconstruction, we should try to discover the underlying principles that rule the current game style of the team. Sometimes these principles are ignored by the players (they don't know what they know). These fundamental principles are based on their experience and the historical and cultural background they had. This is not an obvious process. If the coach is too "mechanism-oriented" he will only attain the top of the iceberg, and doing that he will be missing something more important.

Once the former principles are highlighted, the first question is if we should keep these principles or we should get rid of them. We should try to keep as many principles as we can, because these principles are the substance that conforms the identity of that team. But of course, we should introduce new ones and deactivate some others, if needed.

The next step is to start forging new principles. To forge a new principle requires time, patience and the capacity to seduce the players. First of all you should explain the new principle to your players, explain what and why and convince them. And then you must prepare a good program for the "how". You should start from the source of the principle, in a very micro and simple way, and progressively apply this principle into more complex and global situations. We require a good training program and wise task design.

Once new principles are adopted by our team, the last step is to determine new mechanisms according to the new principles. Mechanisms where those principles will naturally appear. But wait a second, Andreu. Do we need mechanisms beyond our principles? Yes, I claim. They both should coexist. Actually, we should take mechanisms as movement patterns that locate our players in a particular context where they will naturally apply our principles more effectively. For example, if one of my principles is "Hit &

Hope", I should determine a mechanism that allows me to have players in certain areas of the field (from where I would like to smash the circle? how many players do I want there?). I can design a mechanism that creates this desired context where my principle will naturally operate. Following that example: "When we have possession in the opposite half, one of our midfielders should stand in front of the free-man". This mechanism will be in concordance with our "Hit & Hope" principle. This is the proper way to use mechanisms, I claim.

Don't try to establish mechanisms if there is not proper awareness of game principles inside the team. Don't try to build-up a game style only with principles, we also need some spatial rules for certain players. Don't try to impose your "default" set of principles everywhere you go. Don't try to apply new principles without the proper time assimilation process. Preparing mechanisms against your opponent's mechanisms is something wise to do. And finally, try to have different sets of principles with different mechanisms related, so you can variate your style of play depending on the context and opponent. That is probably the last and most difficult stage to achieve!

10 Lessons from Carl Von Clausewitz on Field Hockey

19/10/2018

Today I want to write a text about what war can teach us about our beloved sport. If we speak about war we find several gurus among history that we can't ignore. One of these masters was Carl Von Clausewitz (1780-1831), a prussian general and military theorist who served the prussian army and who suffered two big problems during his life: Napoleon and the cholera. According to history he was a better theorist than general. He left us one of the most important texts about the art of war: "On War" is the creative name of the book that was published in 1932 (posthumously and is actually an unfinished work). I strongly recommend you to read this book if you're a sport nerd or a utopian pacifist. Let's see 10 lessons that we can extract from Von Clausewitz and apply on field hockey:

"To achieve victory we must mass our forces at the hub of all power and movement. The enemy's center of gravity."

Here what Carl tells us is the importance of discovering where the gravity center of our opponent is located and then try to combat it with our specific game plan. For example, if our opponent is really good at attacking the right-hand flank, then we should block this side and channel them to the left side of the pitch. If our opponent is feeling powerful in playing long possessions in our half, we should be able to open a transitional game in order to prevent this "desired" behaviour.

> *"Tactics is the art of using troops in battle; strategy is the art of using battles to win the war"*

True. Strategy goes first, tactics later. Inside a game (war) we must be able to detect and plan different game situations (battles) and try to win them. For example, a game situation can be our high press against their outlet, or our set-pieces in opposite 23. Once we determine these battles we should employ our tactics in order to solve these situations, creating appropriate mechanisms and principles.

> *"Four elements make up the climate of war: danger, exertion, uncertainty and chance."*

Also in hockey. As coaches we must consider these four factors into our game plan. Danger is the capacity that we have to harm our opponent and vice versa. Exertion is the effort done, the work we should do inside the field in order to achieve our objectives. Uncertainty is the nature of our complex sport, nothing can be fully predicted and our players must be ready to deal with these changing situations. And finally chance, which is the awareness of the "windows of opportunities". We must be ready to take the advantage once the chance to take it is given.

"Close combat, man to man, is plainly to be regarded as the real basis of combat."

We shouldn't get lost in macro-structures. At the end, the source of the advantage is the duel. If we have players that are able to directly eliminate opponents, and we have defenders that are hardly eliminated, then we have the fundamental key to succeed in our battles. Every team advantage starts in a form of duel.

"War therefore is an act of violence to compel our opponent to fulfill our will."

In any hockey game there is a battle between two different wills. Two game plans pretending to prevail over the other one. Two teams fighting for the same points. If we are able to submit our opponent to our will, that will be our first step to the final victory. We must force them to follow our game plan. We must take the initiative and force the enemy to play according to our intention, and we must do it through violence, while imposing our principles over them.

"Blind aggressiveness would destroy the attack itself, not the defense."

We shouldn't overestimate passion. To trust in epics should be the last resort in our agenda. Blind aggressiveness in attacking can be counterproductive for the efficiency of the attack itself, causing worse decisions and therefore less rendiment. Rationality must always prevail in attack as well as in and defense.

"Of all the passions that inspire a man in a battle, none, we

have to admit, is so powerful and so constant as the longing for honor and renown."

Honour and renown are the best tools we have as coaches to motivate our players. The social recognition. Everyone loves to feel important and responsible for team success. If we're able to manage these ego rewards properly we will have our army committed and ready to sacrifice themselves for the sake of victory. But alert, that outcome can only be achieved while combining it with hard discipline. The good and the bad cop mantra.

"PRINCIPLE is likewise such a law for action, except that it has not the formal definite meaning, but is only the spirit and sense of law in order to leave the judgment more freedom of application when the diversity of the real world cannot be laid hold of under the definite form of a law."

Von Clausewitz was bold. He was the first one to highlight the distinction between principles and mechanisms (rules). More than ever, our sport must be guided mostly by principles. Principles leave more space for freedom in every decision-making process, and while in hockey the environment is non-linear (as in war), principles will tend to function better than formal instructions and protocols.

"The world has a way of undermining complex plans. This is particularly true in fast moving environments. A fast moving environment can evolve more quickly than a complex plan can be adapted to it. By the time you have adapted, the target has changed."

When everything changes too quickly and variates in an unpredictable way, long and detailed game plans are no longer useful. It makes no sense to spend time and energy in planning complex tactics when we won't be able to deal with unexpected changes that our enemy has prepared for us. Our players must be armed with general principles instead of specific commands.

> "If a segment of one's force is located where it is not sufficiently busy with the enemy, or if the troops are on the march - that is, idle - while the enemy is fighting, then these forces are being managed uneconomically. In this sense they are being wasted, which is even worse than using them inappropriately."

Our prussian hockey lover points out the importance of employing our best players in order to maximize our team performance. It makes no sense to have our resources underemployed. If our best players are not participating enough we should try to do something immediately. It's better to have our best player committing mistakes than having him not touching the ball.

Forging Intelligent Players in 5 Steps

16/11/2018

We want to have intelligent players in our team. As hockey fans we love to watch intelligent players in action. As opponents we hate facing intelligent players. But...wait a second, what is an intelligent player? and, most important, how can we create it? Actually, can we?

Intelligence is the ability to acquire and apply knowledge and skills. The most important words in this definition are the two verbs "acquire" and "apply". A player can "acquire" knowledge and skills independently. But this player firstly needs to have an interpretation kit that tells him/her what to interpret, select and reject. We need a criterion. Therefore, there is always room for education. And it happens something similar with the verb "apply". Once you have the knowledge acquired you should understand how to apply this knowledge into your ordinary practise, in our case, into the hockey game. The proper application requires guidance, practise and feedback.

Forging an intelligent player is a process where coaches have an important role. This text is about forging intelligent players, what to forge and how to do it. The article is made in a form of "5 steps to" because these titles always create more interest, but don't get me wrong, this is a complex process and difficult to achieve. Really difficult.

1. Open Mind

You can't burn wet wood. Some players don't like to be coached. Some believe that they already know everything and interpret every coaching tip as a personal offense. Prepotency and insecurity, both important handicaps for a proper learning mindset. But there are also more subtle habits that jeopardize the learning too.

Sometimes I'm coaching "skills" to individual players, trying to show them how to hit properly, for example. I'm trying to modify swings that have been practised for years, and you can feel how some players don't want to open themselves to the possibility of doing something in a different way. They prefer the known than the unknown. I had a player that during 4 years was hitting the ball with both hands separated at the top of the grip. After 4 years there were hundreds of "hands together" tips but the player never changed it. Difficult instruction to apply? No, just a mental block. Sometimes our minds imprison us under the appearance of self-security. So, first of all, develop in your players the spirit to explore new things and the curiosity to question everything.

2. Contextual Awareness

Every proper application, to be properly applied by the subject, previously requires the knowledge of the context where the application will have to be properly applied (sorry for that). The intelligence of a hockey player must be applied in a hockey context, so the awareness of this context is a *sine qua non* condition for this application. How are we aware of the context? Through our perception. In our game that basically means through our vision. There is no intelligent player without proper vision. Impossible. You can have idiot players with very good vision, but it is impossible to have an intelligent player without good vision. Alert, vision of what? Vision about relevant stimulus . So develop in your players the capacity to be aware of the context through vision, with and without the ball.

3. Risk Management

Once the context is properly perceived now is time to take decisions. Most of the time, the validity of a tactical decision is determined by the risk that implies in its implementation, not by the possible outcome of that decision. For example, facing a 1v4 can be from a tactical point of view a stupidity, even though the player wins that battle. It was a bad decision because the odds to lose the ball were higher than the odds to eliminate the 4 defenders. Intelligent players have the capacity to manage effectively. They are constantly aware of the different situations, possibilities and probabilities coexisting in the field. Where is the superiority? Where should we bring the opponent? How can we prevent danger? What options should I provide to my teammate? This risk management obviously requires a lot of coaching and tactical guidance from the coach.

We must develop this capacity to read the game and we will do it while providing tactical principles and allowing the players to understand why and how to apply them.

4. Game Momentums

Hockey is a battle. This battle is between two teams of 11 members each. This battle is limited in time and measured with a score. These are the three essential variables that intelligent players always take into account when they play. The variation of these variables, in coordination or independently, can produce a variation of the game momentum. For example, if you receive a goal against, that phenomenon will affect the "emotional state" of the team, so this negative impact in the momentum must be well managed.

What do we do if we're winning by one goal, we have one player less and there's just five minutes left to play? What do we do after scoring the 3-0 in the last quarter of a game? Do we go for more goals or we focus on defense and secure the victory? Are we prepared for these decisions? Every intelligent player knows how to deal with momentum but this is not a god's gift quality, this is something that can be discussed, practised and improved during the week. As a coach you should try to develop the capacity to detect game momentums and then take appropriate decisions according to them.

5. Rules

Every sport is constrained by a set of rules. These rules keep the game under some standards and limitate the range of actions that can be executed by the players. The rules are the same for everyone but not everyone manages the rules in the same way. Intelligent players always try to get an advantage out of the rules. For example, you can play a quick restart in order to eliminate your direct opponent. There are many small stratagems that intelligent players use in order to get advantages out of the rules. There's a fine line between these astute tricks and unethical behaviours, I admit it. For example, asking for a foot when you know that it wasn't foot, celebrating a goal when you didn't touch the ball or winning a bully when the opponent previously had the possession of the ball. These controversial actions are not addressed by my proposal here.

Intelligent players understand how to manipulate the opponent with a wise use of the rules. This intelligent ability also works with umpires. Intelligent players invest time and energy in having good relations with umpires. In the long run it is always better to have the respect and trust from the umpires. Always. So, try to develop the capacity to gain advantage out of the rules and also the capacity to seduce umpires.

If you achieve players with these 5 capacities you will have intelligent players inside the field. But remember that Utopia is not a reality. In practise you will always have some players that are capable to become intelligent players and some others that, due to other reasons, will always be a bit dumb inside the field. With this second set of players make sure that they obey and don't think a lot! No, seriously, our obligation as coaches is to establish a working philosophy that provides the chance to develop to everyone, but be ready to accept some degree of failure. Human nature is complex and our range of possibilities is limited.

Looking for Control in a VUCA Game

22/11/2018

VUCA is an acronym introduced by the US Army War College in 1987. It describes the Volatility, Uncertainty, Complexity and Ambiguity of the contemporary world in comparison with the modern world before the end of the cold war. Well, this VUCA concept is having an impact in many other human spheres including the sport. And from my perspective, also in the way that field hockey is played today. Let's see the main characteristics of our VUCA in hockey:

Volatile: *"The volatility refers to the different situational social-categorization of people due to specific traits or reactions that stand out during that particular situation" (Wikipedia).* In our sport this social-categorization can be translated into "positions". Today we're not able to predict how a particular player will react given a particular context. We see defenders running forward, strickers dropping back and midfielders everywhere. Former categorized-identities are disappearing. Players are being much more versatile.

Uncertain: *"Uncertainty may occur in the intention to imply causation or correlation between the events of a social perceiver and a target." (Wikipedia).* Teams are adopting new game styles while constantly surprising the opponents. For example, we have seen Germany playing a high zone and India playing conservational game. That is something impossible to imagine 10 years ago. We can no longer predict how a particular team is going to play, how they are going to execute their set-pieces or which players are going to be selected in the squad.

Complex: *"That refers to the interconnectivity and interdependence of multiple components in a system." (Wikipedia).* Due to the rise of technology and science nowadays we're able to collect a huge amount of information regarding performance: from videos to gps, from physiology to psychology. The variables that influence the final performance of our athletes are multiple, interdependent and interconnected.

Ambiguous: *"This refers to when the general meaning of something is unclear even when an appropriate amount of information is provided." (Wikipedia).* Everytime we find fewer and fewer "big personalities" on the field, and we have more and more ambiguous players. You never know what these guys really want. The "Z Generation" is living in a virtual world, lacking some interpersonal abilities and collaboration spirit. It is difficult to approach them, because they operate in a very different way that we do as coaches. They seem ambiguous to us. Now the next logical question is: given this context, what do we do as coaches? How can we train our teams in a VUCA environment? I'm going to start explaining how not to do it. The way we pretend to deal within a VUCA game is through the aim of control. How do we manifest this aim of control in our daily coaching practises?

We bomb our players with commands: The joystick coach. From the bench we try to rule the game and players' decisions. We can't cope with players acting in a volatile way. We feel that our contribution from the sideline is crucial in the quality of the game played. When there's a mistake, we think about how we can prevent it next time. When there's a successful action due to our command then we feel happy. This behaviour incapacitate the players and overstress the coach.

We design infinite plans: A plan, but also B,C,D and E, depending on what the opponent does, the score, the time, the numbers, the weather, the umpires and the moon. In order to deal with uncertainty our aim is to plan every possible scenario in advance. If we have enough plans we will always be able to keep the situation under control, we believe. Do you know the reason why coaches spend most of the time talking about outlets and press? Because these two static situations are easy to plan and control.

We get horny with science: If we agree that processes are complex, then let's collect as much data as we can! There is a study that proves the positive correlation between drinking coffee before the game and performance, so let's drink coffee before the game! There is another study proving that chewing gum reduces stress in athletes during warm-ups, so let's give chewing gums to our players! There is a new software that is able to predict risk injury rates taking into account the date of the calendar. The aim of control makes people addicted to science. And this is a never ending story.

We impose our domination: The aim of controlling our players makes us act as micro dictators. We can't tolerate ambiguous behaviours. You're with or against me. We define rules to follow and we are really strict if someone is not fitting the predetermined shape. When we make selections we prefer docile sheep than furious wolves. We struggle when we have to face a conflict and manage it face to face. We prefer to negate or suppress it.

This aim for control is condemned to failure for two reasons: it can't be successful and it destroys the coach. It can't be successful because the world is VUCA, so by definition it can't be fully controlled. The impossibility to control the game makes the aim of control something stupid and useless. So what do we do if we can't control our game? Try to influence it. The difference between control and influence is crucial. Influence is focused on long-term, control is focused on short-term. Influence through principles, control through commands. Influence is about empowering, control is about claiming credit. Influence is about taking care of others, control is only about yourself.

And it can't be successful because it destroys the coach. The aim of control can easily become an obsession. And any obsession is harmful for one's health. One of the most common pathologies in coaches is anxiety. Anxiety takes place when coaches feel that the more time they spend in "controlling" processes, the better outcomes they get. Believing that naturally generates the need to do more and more, but this is an endless battle (because you could always do more). You should cultivate "acceptance". Be happy with a 6 or 7 and don't go always for a 10. Or that obsession will gradually destroy you. In order to avoid this high level of anxiety it is very important to delegate responsibilities among the rest of your staff and players. Don't try to control everything. Accept that your resources are limited and accept that there are too many variables to control in a hockey game.

We can't control a VUCA game. The only thing that we can do is to influence the game. Try to reproduce VUCA environments in your training sessions and try to develop the capacity to deal within this context. Trust your team, your staff and spread responsibilities.

Coach, you're not that important.

Superiorities, from the Chessboard to the Field

10/01/2019

In hockey, like in any other field of knowledge, there are many famous terms that are commonly used. Terms that sound nice and fit well in any sentence. For example, in the Netherlands they use the word "energy" as one of these lexic jokers. You say something like "the energy was not good enough" or "great energy, guys" and everyone agrees and thinks how good you are. If we specifically talk about hockey tactics, there are also some magic concepts like the one that represents the object of this text: **the superiority or advantage**. What do we mean by finding superiority? Exploiting superiority? Create numerical or positional superiorities? Generate advantage? I hope this text can bring some light on that.

For this purpose I'm going to use some ideas extracted from the exciting sport of chess (chess is a sport although you can't buy a chessboard at Decathlon) and I'll try to transfer these ideas into our hockey field. In chess they have been studying the concept of superiority / advantage for centuries. And they have defined some different types of "advantage" that we can also use in hockey.

First-move Advantage

It's been statistically proven that starting to play with whites brings more odds to win than starting with blacks. The average is slightly above 50% but it's constantly proven tournament after tournament. For example, during the last Hockey World Cup in India, out of 36 games, there was a winner in 27 of them (draws are not counted). Out of these 27 games with a single winner, in 21 of them, the first team that scored was the final winner of the game. So in hockey scoring first increases your odds to win the game as well.

Quantitative Material Advantage

In chess there is a quantitative material advantage when you have more pieces than your opponent on the chessboard. In hockey we use the concept of "Numerical Superiority". We have a numerical superiority when we're more than our opponent. This is clear when there is a time suspension due to a card but the meaning goes beyond this particular moment. When players with potential participation in the action are more than the number of opponents, then we have a numerical superiority in that context. We can have numerical superiorities while attacking or defending. For longer or shorter periods of time.

Qualitative Material Advantage

If the number of pieces is equal, the absolute value of the pieces can be different depending on the particular value of the pieces that you have. For example, it's not the same to have a bishop and a knight (value of 6), than having a rook and a knight (value of 8). In this case, the second player has a "quality of advantage" over the first one. In hockey we use the term "Qualitative Superiority" for that. We have this superiority when we're better than our opponents in a given context. That means that our players are able to execute the actions with more effectiveness than our opponents. So, given a numerical equality, we will have a qualitative superiority if our players directly involved in the action are better than the direct opponents. Actually, we could have an extreme situation: we could have a qualitative superiority and a numerical inferiority at the same time. Indeed, if you have Robert Kemperman, Valentin Verga and Seve van As together, they will be hard to stop even with your 11 players!

Positional Advantage

While the material advantage is based on the absolute value of the pieces, the positional advantage is based on its relative value. It's based on the "potency" of these pieces regarding its position on the chessboard and their possible actions according to their positions. Potency is determined by time and space. When a player has spatial advantage is when their pieces have a better position on the chessboard than the pieces of the opponent. Better means that we're able to protect and threaten more spaces than our opponent. The time advantage is related to the number of movements that you have to execute before achieving a particular space. You will have a positional advantage if the time you spend is less than the time that your opponent needs to spend in order to achieve or protect the same space.

In hockey we use the concept of "Positional Superiority". We have this superiority when we are better placed than our opponents in a given context. Our players are located in a way that disables the successful participation of the opponents. This better placement is related to the space and time, but also related to the body position and the field of vision.

Combinational Advantage

In chess, a seqüence of movements is called "combination". Every combination has the goal to create any type of advantage. The combination emerges from the interaction between different pieces. Out of their potencies combined. Obviously, every combination is coherent with a plan that is in the player's mind, because pieces are not autonomous agents. Depending on the position of the pieces and the ability of the master to combine them, we will have better potential combinations that will harm the opponent more or less.

In hockey, this concept is called "Socio-Affective Superiority". We have this superiority when we relate better than our opponent. That is related to the identity of our players and their "connecting capital" . For example, if we're in a 2v2 situation where there is no qualitative advantage and no positional advantage, we can still generate an advantage if our players are able to coordinate themselves successfully, for instance, with a perfect give and go combination.

As we have seen, there is a close relation between all the possible advantages in chess and the theory of superiorities (Seirul·lo) applied in hockey. Most of the "old paradigm" coaches are only focused on finding numerical superiorities, which is quite complicated to achieve. It's perhaps better to focus more on the other 3 superiorities because they are easier to generate during the game.

First of all, try to improve the skills of your players, so they will have higher value and, given equal situations, they'll tend to be better than your opponents. Second, try to show them where, when and how to be preferentially placed inside the field, so they will take the advantage of positional superiority often. And finally, develop their capacity to relate well between each other, so they will combine better than their opponents.

Parking the Bus in Hockey

07/02/2019

How many times have we heard: "Against this team you better park the bus or you'll lose" or "park the bus and make sure you don't receive goals against"? These two reasons are built upon a premise: parking the bus reduces the odds to receive goals against. Well, I'll try to argue why in hockey this premise is fallacious.

We like to compare our sport with football. That usually works for most of the comparisons but sometimes not. Our sport has some singularities that make it different from football too. So once we compare both sports, we should firstly think about that comparison.

What is "parking the bus"?

Parking the bus is an expression coined by the great José Mourinho in 2004 after drawing a game 0-0 against Tottenham. The spurs decided to defend with 8 players in front of the circle and they were successful in frustrating all the offensive attempts from Chelsea. Since then, the expression is commonly used when there is a team who deploys most of the players low in the field while defending their circle. However, besides "parking the bus" we have other expressions that share the same meaning, for example the italian "catenaccio" famously practised by the same Mourinho against FCBarcelona in the Champions League 2010 semi-final.

Why can "parking the bus" be successful in football?

If you deploy 8 or 9 defenders in front of the circle you increase the density. This crowded area prevents the opponent from having enough space and time to combine and shoot on target from a good position. The football ball is very big in comparison with the legs of the players, and in football you are allowed to stop the ball with your legs, therefore it becomes really difficult to get something productive when there is a huge number of legs surrounding the ball. Moreover, consider that in football you have the "off-side" rule that creates a forbidden zone at the back of the last defender, that is something that still reduces more space for the attackers.

Against this "parking the bus" defences, teams start shooting from longer distances and crossing balls from the sides, both solutions can be dangerous but you must have the right players to do that. Teams like FCBarcelona became great experts in disarming "buses" with short passing combinations, but this is a mastery that is not accessible to everyone. If you have Leo Messi you can disarm anything.

But why is "parking the bus" less successful in hockey?

In hockey you don't have off-side, you can spot players deep to the baseline. That pushes the opponent lower and inside the circle. If there are defenders already placed inside the circle, there are less players available to eventually prevent the circle approximation and penetration. As attackers, if we stretch the field with our back 4 really wide, opposite strikers can't cover this enormous space, that back 4 width generates time and space for the ball carrier (normally one of the central defenders) and increases the capacity to play good balls inside the circle. Take into account that most of the times the free-man is usually down inside the circle as well.

Also we should take into consideration that the hockey ball is small and you can only stop it with the stick, which is small too, that makes the ball interception more difficult than in football. And if there is a free-hit close to the circle, using self-pass, any player can be easily eliminated while conceding easy circle penetrations. But that's not all. Once the ball is inside the circle there is always the risk to commit a penalty corner (lots of feet inside the circle), which is a clear goal chance. Crowding low defensive areas is not the best idea in hockey.

Parking the bus in hockey has too many risks and disadvantages compared to football. The closer from the circle your team stands the more circle penetrations, penalty corners and goal chances you will invariably concede. Therefore it's not the best idea to voluntarily park the bus. I said "voluntarily" because sometimes teams are irremediably forced to park the bus against their will. That happens because most of the teams prefer to keep the free-man low and inside the circle, so they can't cope with the superiority from the opponent back 4. That is something that naturally pushes the team low and low and finally you park the bus when that wasn't your intention.

How to avoid that?

We should start pushing our free-man higher in these situations while creating an "all-man-to-man" context. Remove the "libero" from the cave and put ball pressure everywhere. If your team becomes an expert on that defensive resource, you can even park the bus as a deception tool and then surprise your opponent with surprising press and productive fast breaks, but that's a different story.

"Parking the bus" can be successful in football. It's less effective in hockey. But it's always ugly, don't you think?

Sharing is Caring

18/02/2019

Last week there was a twitter feed initiated by the friend Bernardo Fernandes about how social media can help coaches. After his question -open to everyone-, a cyber-exchange of tweets started. Some very good coaches were interpelled and they exposed their opinions and shared some interesting comments about the topic of discussion. There were comments, camaraderie and some desires, like the convenience to create new exchange platforms that could allow these top coaches to share information, knowledge and experiences among them.

I was very happy to see how these role models were expressing opinions on twitter, interpellating each other and allowing "the others" to contemplate their opinions with chances to participate in the conversation. It's always nice to see how these brilliant minds think and would be great to see them more engaged in "public" discussions on social media. Twitter is the perfect platform to do that.

I still remember when Max Caldas visited us during the last FIH Coaching Course. He came and decided to stand in front of the class and he said: "Ok guys, what do you want to know?. That's all. He was 100% transparent about tactics, problems in the squad, training methodology, etc...For more than one hour we had a top coach answering our doubts. This is "sharing" in its pure. No need to hide stuff behind nice powerpoint presentations. I also remember a long time ago when in a coaching course in Catalonia, after a class about tactics, a young student went to the professor with this question: "Teacher, aren't you afraid of sharing what you're doing with your team?", and the teacher said "No, because what I know is not mine", he answered before leaving the room.

How stupid was that answer, right? Of course what we know is ours. We've been working really hard to know what we know now! And as coaches our value is our knowledge! If I share this knowledge with everyone how can I prevent my competitors from overcoming me? If I share what I know with others how can I make sure that I keep my value in my hockey institution? If I'm not the owner of any particular and exclusive idea, then what's my singular value proposition? In the end I have to protect my job, no?

How stupid was last paragraph, right? What I know is due to what I've learned, and If I have learned something it is because of my experience, ergo thanks to my narration, ergo thanks to my interpretations, ergo my language, ergo my culture....and the culture is something that is produced and shared constantly by everyone. And the same process with all the books read courses attended or interesting conversations kept. Knowledge is a social activity. The intellectual capital is expressed through interaction, not through its possession. To accumulate knowledge doesn't have any utility. And my value as a coach is my complex uniqueness, product of infinite variables (attitude, skills, values…). My value is not a bunch of diagrams, drills and vídeos stored in a hard drive.

Probably most of you agree in this first thesis, which is: knowledge should be shared, not possessed. However, the crucial question is far from being touched yet. Big problems appear when we try to extend the sentence with…"shared with whom?" "how", "when" and "why". There are always two opposite forces engaged when we talk about sharing knowledge between peers. The first force pushes the coach to share his ideas with others, seduce them and get their recognition and admiration. Referring to Nietzsche and his concept of "Will of Power", that is expansion. The other force pulls the coach away from open discussions, preventing the possibility to be overtaken by others. That is conservation.

Let's suppose that there is a discussion between two coaches. These two coaches are both "masters" in their respective contexts, so there is a subtle and mutual interest in being recognized and "desired" by the other. Both coaches unconsciously desire the submission of the other coach when they discuss hockey. Here submission means something like: "you're right, mate". Their desire is to feel that they know more than the other. Discussions as dialectical battles. And there is always a winner of these battles: the one with less fear to lose (I won't go deeper here). This coach, the winner of the contest, becomes the new master in this particular relation of power, and the other coach becomes the new subdued subject ("slave" in hegelian terms).

This Hegelian dynamic is specially present in staff, between head coach and assistants. Normally the head coach is the master. The head coach subdues the assistant. The problem is that once the assistant becomes the "slave" in this relation, the joy of the master is over because there is no joy in being recognized by a slave. The joy must always come from the recognition of another master.

These big coaches are always surrounded by a group of coaches who really work hard (they are the ones that truly create the culture, Hegel would say) while the master receives all the recognition from the public. This hard-work, paradoxically, is what makes the slave more human than the master, who passively gets fat in praise. This responsibility towards material work becomes formative for the slave *(bildung)*, while the master goes into decline within this passive authority role.

So, what is the desire of the master once he has subdued his close slaves? To extend his power and subue more individuals while aiming for more recognition. If coaches aim for more recognition, they have to submit other "masters", as we said earlier. Therefore, coaches are unconsciously attracted to meet other coaches and have dialectical battles with them, so they can find more food for their ego.

The beautiful side of dialectics is that most of the time occurs in a is subte, fine and smooth way. All these processes are commonly taking place under the shape of political correctness with mutual acceptance. Hegel defined the master-slave dialectic as the common engine in all human relations, from the individual to the society as a whole (then Karl Marx took over). Like Fractals, the same dynamic operates everywhere. When a bunch of experts want to create such a "knowledge hub", what they actually want to do is to delimit a new area "just for top coaches" that will automatically create new other underprivileged subjects that will be obviously excluded from this "elite" group.

Initially these elitist entities bring joy to its members, because their members feel special and exclusive, like the aristocrats of *"The Exterminating Angel" (Luis Buñuel, 1962)* enjoying the fest. But this addictive bourgeois joy invariably turns into violence and decadence. It's just a matter of time. Violence because Hegel will naturally appear creating fratricides dialectical battles forming new masters and slaves within the group. And decadent because there is no sustainable innovation from endogamy. The "top coaching panel" becomes the new precious *"Beach" (Danny Boyle, 2000)*, a secret paradise for some selected coaches. A paradise that will end in hell.

If social media has brought something good, that is the capacity to allow massive interaction between people from all over the world and with very different profiles. A huge intellectual capital is available to everyone. If we want to extend our knowledge there is only one way to do it: sharing what we know with others and therefore accepting the possibility to be "exposed", that is, being able to be interpelled by everyone. If we want to extend the knowledge of hockey and innovate together, let's get engaged in wider and open discussions. Let's share what we think and keep the discussion door open to everyone. If you like to read tweets from wise thinkers then start writing yours as well.

Let's create more sharing platforms like the one done by Bernardo Fernandes (Self-Pass), Javier Telechea (Coaching Hockey) or Ernst

Baart (HockeyTodayCC). Let's discuss, interact and challenge others and their ideas! Socrates was named the "gadfly of Athens" because he was constantly challenging people in the streets.

It's better to be exposed at the arena than to be hidden in a cave, even in a precious cave.

Hockey from the Paradigm of Complexity

07/03/2019

In 1928, the german biologist Karl Ludwig von Bertalanffy launched the "Theory of Systems". This new scientific paradigm was based on the study of the interrelations between the elements of a system. Prior to this contribution the mantra was to believe that the behaviour of systems was the addition of its elements, therefore that systems could be well studied solely from the analysis of its separated parts. That was the old mechanistic paradigm.

But in the paradigm of complexity, all the constitutive elements of a system are dependent on each other, therefore the study of these interrelations becomes crucial. This new theory was initially applied to science but later on also to social spheres. And recently also in sport. In the present text we will try to approach the field hockey phenomenon from this paradigm of complexity.

"When we try to understand things systematically that means literally to put them in a certain context and establish the nature of its relations." Fritjof Capra

A hockey team as a system has different characteristics:

- Is Open: The team and the players are constantly exchanging information with the context.

- Is Abstract: The team is ruled by symbolic patterns or concepts (principles).

- Is Complex: It is constituted by multiple interrelations.

- Is Dynamic: It constantly evolves/changes through time.

- Is Non-Linear: Its behavior is not predictable.

- Is Chaotic: Small changes in the inputs can generate big changes in the outputs.

- Is Adaptative: It adapts itself to the context

The fundamental element of a hockey system is the player. However, the player is itself a complex system, emerging from the interrelation between different dimensions/structures. As coaches we should take into consideration these structures and how they interrelate between each other in order to optimize the performance of our player. According to Paco Seirul·lo, these are the six structures that configure the complex nature of the player:

- Conditional: the physical structure (strength, endurance, speed…)

- Coordinative: the coordination and the motor skills execution (technique)

- Cognitive: how to process information and take decisions inside the field (tactical mindset)

- Socio-Affective: the interpersonal relations between players, the capacity to connect/understand each other on and off the field.

- Emotive-Volitional: the self identity, the personal will transferred into assertiveness, proactivity and mental strenght against difficulties.

- Creative-Expressive: the capacity to innovate during the game

If we understand the player as a complex system itself, when we prepare our training session we should integrate these six dimensions in every task. Although we can put the focus mainly in one of them (for example in decision-making), we should take into consideration the remaining ones and make sure they are also present. Basically, we should try not to remove structures while preparing our tasks, because the normal game already contains everything.

The player is an autonomous agent but inside the field he/she should follow certain behavioural standards (tactical principles). If not, there won't be a unique identity as a system. From this perspective, it is mandatory the creation of a certain level of "order" emerging from the natural chaos of the game. This order is what we call the "Game Model". The game model should respect the natural synergies between players and its characteristics, but should also set certain principles that will guide their behavior inside the field. The paradigm of complexity defines these principles as "attractors". The complex system tends to stabilize around certain attractors. These attractors are patterns that describe the behavior of the system though time. These principles orientate conducts while setting preferential collective behaviors.

How do we define these principles?

We should do it while attending the nature of our players and their spontaneous interrelations. We should not bring our set of principles from home when we start coaching a new team. First we should observe what actually emerges between them and then make our proposal.

And how do we organize these principles?

We should have different principles in every game phase: attacking, defending and both transitions. But be careful, these principles should be coherent and compatible between them. For example, if one of our principles in attack is to constantly play long balls, then we can't have the principle of press after loss because this way of attacking naturally spreads the team and reduces the density, which is something needed in press after loss moments. There must be harmony between all the principles. In other words: in every attractor we should have the presence of the whole model.

A team that is playing without any Game Model is a team where its behaviours are random, so the system can't hardly show any collective attitude and players can't interrelate effectively. However, the Game Model must be flexible. We shouldn't constrain too much the actions of our players, we should only try to guide them. If a Game Model is too restrictive our team will become predictable and less adaptive to new circumstances. In the process of setting the Game Model we should try to balance individual and collective interests. Our Model should integrate different wills, potentialities, naturalities, talents, emotions, knowledge and individual expectations. If not, it will be seen as something imposed from outside, and we don't want that.

And how do we prepare our team for this complex nature?

While training close to the chaos. Sometimes we interpret chaos as disorder. That is not true. Chaos is the instability in the process of stability, it's a dynamic process. Our training should contain continuous changes in the context so the players should constantly self-organize and adapt.

Most of the time we prepare training tasks where the natural complexity of our sport is not present. That makes no sense. Every task should contain the fundamentals of our sport: which is the presence of the stick and ball, the presence of team mates, the presence of opponents and the presence of both goals (progression and threat). We also need to have the presence of time and score (competition). But that's not all, we also need the eventual variation of numbers (inferiority, superiority). The more we can disrupt the equilibrium the better. When the team self-organizes in front of a changing environment and gets used to apply different principles, the system evolves. We require this level of variability if we want to optimize our team and our players.

Between order and chaos there is complexity. The generation of this "ordered chaos", the synergies between players, the development of attractors and the variability in our training session will demand new coaching staffs with professionals from different disciplines able to work in a coordinated and integrated way.

The staff shouldn't be a fractionator of the reality; the staff should be the manager of complexity.

Designing Small-Sided Games

03/04/2019

I already wrote about how Hockey is conceived from the paradigm of complexity. This new paradigm, besides bringing a new interpretation of the game and its characteristics, it also implies a new way of thinking about the training methodology. Here I'm going to give my opinion about how a "complex" training session should look like and how to design proper Small-Sided Games (SSG) where we can apply the principles of our Game Model (GM).

First of all, my proposal tries to distinguish the two main training methodologies regarding the nature of the task. We have the "analytic" method, where the goal is to focus on a particular aspect of the game in a "isolated" way. And we have the "integrated/global" method, where different skills are practised simultaneously in a more realistic environment. Should we choose one of them and discard the other? No. So how should we combine these two methods in our routine? We should combine both methods. But this combination should be done under certain conditions.

The Analytic method is ideal for "Skill Acquisition", that is, the execution of a certain technical action. Hockey is a very demanding sport from a motor skill perspective. And players should dominate a wide range of skills. If not, there will be coordinative limitations that will hinder the final performance of the player. Under the paradigm of complexity, skills should be practised with the use of variability and uncertainty factors (that can also include decision-making). The final goal here is to improve the kinesthetic sense of the individual.

We should avoid the old-paradigm-drills where players are simply repeating and repeating the same skill without any turbulence. Also those drills where players were just following a predetermined succession of actions. That is boring and doesn't work, sorry. These analytic motor skill tasks should be driven by experts and executed in very small groups, ideally individualized. All the players are subject to work on skills, from my young nephew to King Arthur van Doren.

The Integrated/Global method is the ideal for "all the rest", the ideal for the majority of our training time. This method uses the SSG as a main tool. Therefore, if we want to prepare good training sessions we should understand how to design a proper SSG. Here there is a short list of some important factors to consider:

4 Phases: Every task should include the 4 natural phases of the game. That is: attack, defensive transition, defense and offensive transition. For example, if you design a drill where the action is over when defenders regain the ball, this represents a loss in complexity that doesn't fit the true logic of the game. That's why I don't recommend "wave drills".

Rules: If we focus on the press after-loss, we should adapt the rules of the SSG in order to enhance this preferential behaviour, for example: getting a point if you regain the ball in the same zone where you lost it. The rules (rewards in this case) should be designed according to the objective.

Context: Size & shape of the field and player density (nºplayers/m2). These variables should be also designed in coordination with the tactical principles that you want to practise. For example, playing a 5v5 in a half of the field will create different behaviours than if you play the same 5v5 in a quarter of the field. Another variable to consider is the duration of the sets and the rest periods. Playing with full rest (game time equals rest time) creates a different effect than playing with half rest (game time doubles rest time).

Numbers: We should also consider the possibility to use joker/s (extra players who always support the ball possession), or just play with constant asymmetries. Even numbers generate more stress and mental fatigue in our players (less time & space in our decision making). Jokers can be fixed in certain zones or can move freely. Jokers can switch teams every time there is a transition or depending on certain achievements.

Chaos: You can also integrate different SSG all-in-one. That generates "chaos" and stresses the players with more complexity.

For example, you can play a normal 4v4 with 2 goals but suddenly you can switch the validity of these goals to another 4 small goals that are spotted on the sides. And again, all of a sudden you can change that validity to a normal possession game where 5 passes in a row is a point. Depending on what of the three "mini-game" you're playing, there will be different tactical decisions gaining relevance and some others becoming useless. The aim is to create chaos and force our players to constantly adapt.

Principles: You can also play a normal game and put the focus on certain principles, for example: "every time there is a successful give and go you get 1 point". Another example, "we only do press after loss if previously played more than three short passes in that area". When we design the SSG we should define what principle we want to practise. That preferential behaviour can be supported by specific rules/rewards or just by directing the attention of the players.

Competition: In every SSG there must be a competition. Competition implies: a way to score goals/points and a way to avoid the opponent to do it. The goals can be scored to normal goals with goalkeepers, to mini goals or just after accomplishing some requirements (like crossing a line, for example). The presence of the result is always relevant in connection with the presence of time. Therefore, we should inform the players about the duration of the game and the score. And both teams should "compete" according to these variables as well. If your players are not intrinsically competitive enough you can create material or symbolic rewards or punishments, but that is not the ideal situation.

As we can see, there are many dimensions and variables that we should take into consideration when we design a proper SSG. I'm sure that if we start considering these factors more and more, the final outcome will be nice, funny and productive for our team!

Let's think, design and then....let them play!

Complexity in Training Sessions

19/09/2019

The old paradigm

There is still a lot to achieve in the way we design our training sessions. I think we're still not understanding how we can effectively influence the natural complexity of our sport. In most of the cases the way we try to address the game is the classical one, based on a "scientist-mechanistic" approach. Under that old paradigm our aim is to break the game in smaller parts that are easier to detect and understand for the players. Then we make them reproduce and repeat situations in a form of protocol.

This is pure reductionism. A complex reality is not the addition of its parts. What the analytic training is doing, when it separates and isolates is, in essence, faking the true reality of hockey. It's not only that this training methodology is less productive, the bigger problem is that it harms the development capacity of our players. According to the philosopher Edgar Morin, there are four principles that every "simplifier though" applies:

Disjunction: Tends to take the different phenomenon in a separate way, independent from each other. Therefore, the relations between different objects are hidden. In hockey we can find drills where there is no opposition, for example. Or drills where the action finishes when defenders regain the ball.

Reduction: Tends to explain the whole reality attending only one of its constitutive elements. For example, when we say that we lost due to our poor physical condition and then we decide to spend hours and hours running shuttles away from the hockey field. That is reductionism.

Abstraction: Tends to reach general conclusions but unknowing the real origin of them. Under this principle we have coaches that adopt patterns of movement seen in other teams hoping to reproduce the same behaviours in our team. Ignoring the complex nature of behaviours.

Causality: Tends to conceive the reality as a simple cause-effect succession of events. These coaches believe that the whole game can be broken down in multiple sequences of movements. When the center defender passes the ball, the left defender goes wide, then left mid come closer, then right mid go deep, etc...That doesn't work.

Training under Complexity

On the contrary, the new paradigm states that game is not a fully organized dimension where "chaos" is an exception, but a chaotic and uncertain reality with some emergent episodes of order. Under this new focus, training sessions must respect these characteristics (Raffaele Di Pasquale):

The Relations of the Elements: Every task should contain the 4 constitutive phases of the game: attack, defensive transition, defense, offensive transition. For example, the drills based on different "attacking waves" where some players are attackers and some others are defenders are poor and too simplistic.

Global Perceptions: The interpretation of the game must consider the phase of the game, momentum, time, result, etc. The validity of every action is dependent on its context. For example, quick counterattack is not always something desirable. Its judgement should consider potential dangers, emotional state of the team, physical demands, result, etc. Let's cultivate broader perceptions that take more inputs into account.

The "whole player": Every training task should respect the 6 structures of the player: conditional, coordinative, cognitive, socio-affective, emotional-volitive and creative (Paco Seirul·lo). The main objective of your task can be one of these structures, for example, a particular physical load of work, but the other 5 structures must be present as well. The 6 structures are always active when we play the game, so basically the question for the coaches will be not how to include them but how not to exclude some of them when we design our tasks.

Real context: Two different teams with a critical zone to defend and with a high reward zone where to attack. Teams should cooperate among them and compete against each other. Ball possession is constantly changing and all the players can participate in the game. And after a certain period of time the team with the highest score is the winner. This is how our real context is. So try to respect that in every training task that you design. If you do not respect this logic, you are preparing players for a different activity, not for hockey.

Work close to the ZPD: Zone of proximal development (Lev Vygotzky). Challenge your players constantly. Try to push them out of their comfort zone. If a particular task becomes too easy for them, design a new situation where they must fail, grow and learn again. Guide them to that ZPD with the use of your social abilities and motivation tools.

Discovery Learning: Don't treat your players as robots. It's not providing solutions that you will forge an intelligent team. Let them discover the solutions by themselves. Try to stimulate their reasoning with provocative statements, paradoxes and intriguing questions. Let them ponder the risks and benefits of every alternative, and let them discover the validity of their actions, instead of being you the only one who judges them all the time.

Decision Making: In every training task decision-making must be enabled. The wider is the field of possibilities, the richer is the context. If you prepare a 1v1 inside a 10 meters-width channel, there is almost no decision making possible. But if you create a 4v4 game, players will have different passing lines to play combinations or choose 1v1 actions, defenders will have to manage press, interceptions, closing , channeling, etc...The situation as a whole is much more complex, so richer for player's development.

Cognitive Load of Work: If we prepare a good training session under the new paradigm of complexity, we should also manage the cognitive load of work applied to our players. Stress is the natural response of our brain when the situation is complex and there is pressure, fatigue, decisions, rewards and failures. Manage this variable as well. You can also design different tasks with less cognitive fatigue that can still be productive for the development of the team.

I've been talking to different coaches about this topic of complexity in training sessions. There is a common reaction among some of them, something like: "Ok Andreu, so let's play games all the time, no? Easy! ", but with a strange burlesque tone, like if they were losing their predominant power while accepting that the best teacher is the game.

Indeed, most of our training tasks must be small sided games, but that is not just throwing a ball and letting them play freely. Training field is not just a playground. We need the presence of our game model. The "how" we want to play.

Our main responsibility as coaches is how to generate the
appropriate propensities within our small-sided games.

Ode to the Obvious

24/10/2019

Sometimes it is funny to question obvious things about life. It is always in the reign of the obvious where radical ideas emerge (Slavoj Zizek). Yesterday, after the sacred siesta I was drinking a cup of tea on my balcony when I started to reflect about the nature of our beloved sport. Here are some of the obvious questions and obviated answers that I found.

What is a "team"?

The concept of "cooperation" immediately came into my mind. If we play together, that means that we should cooperate towards a common goal, right? For any kind of cooperation I see two necessary ingredients: to have the same goal and to have a common behaviour. But the goal is always the same for everyone: "to win the match", so the crucial ingredient is the second one: how we play together, how we coordinate our actions inside the field. This shared criteria that guides our actions inside the field is what constitutes us as a team. This is the way we play: our game style is what we are as a team.

What is an "opponent"?

Here the word "scarcity" appeared. Two teams fighting for a scarce resource: the ball. The fight for the single ball is what converts "the other" into an opponent. A hockey game with two balls would allow collusion, but that can't happen in our sport. The ball represents the precious object of desire for both teams. Therefore, only the fact of having ball possession is something that hurts the opponent's desire and aspiration. So ball possession has an intrinsic and absolute value. But at the same time, ball possession is not an end itself but a means. The final goal for both teams is to have the highest score after the regular time, and that brought me to the next question.

Why is scoring so important?

We win the game when the number of goals that we scored is higher than the number of goals scored by the opponent. The first logical conclusion is that, at least, we have to score one goal if we want to win a game, so attacking will always be crucial in "winning the game". In other words, you can't win if you only defend. You can't lose if you never concede a goal against, that's true. But "not-losing" is not the essential aim of the game.

And again, if we agree that possession has an intrinsic value, attacking is not only better in terms of maximizing the possibilities to win, it is also a better activity to do, because it's pleasant for you and painful for the opponent. Therefore we can state that the attacking scope of the game should always prevail over defending. Then I went deeper into these two concepts of attacking and defending. The difficulty of the questions were in crescendo.

What is attacking?

It's difficult because in the essence of attacking (what we do when we have the ball), there are two drives coexisting: the will to score a goal and the fear of losing the ball. Therefore I find it almost impossible to have a unique behaviour when we attack, considering these two forces. How do we attack? If we are guided by the drive to score a goal, the progression becomes the main attractor here because the circle is at the end of the opponent's field. If we are guided by the fear of losing the ball, the ball maintenance becomes the main attractor, simply because if you have the ball the opponent can't have it. Teams should know how to play under these two different drives. But wait, unless there is an existing way to synthesize both positions. As coaches we should try to find the most effective way to progress in the field while keeping good control of the ball.

What is defending?

A similar freudian dichotomy exists in the concept of defending: when we defend there are also two drives fighting for its power: the will to regain the ball (and have the possibility to attack) and the impulse to defend our circle and avoid the scoring chance from the opponent. How do we defend? If we are driven by the will of "regaining", we are going to chase the ball, press the opponent and try to recover as soon as possible. If we are guided by the will to defend our circle, we will drop back close to our goal, reduce the space to defend and make sure that the opponent doesn't have enough time and space to reach our circle and generate a goal chance. But wait, unless there is a possible way to merge both drives. As coaches we should try to find the most effective way to quickly regain the ball while disallowing the progression of the opponent.

Everything sounds quite obvious after reading it again:

- The shared criterion that guides our actions inside the field is what constitutes us as a team. The way we play: our game style is what we are.

- Ball possession has an intrinsic and absolute value.

- Attacking scope should always prevail over defending.

- In attacking, try to find the most effective way to progress in the field while keeping good control of the ball.

- In defense, find the most effective way to quickly regain the ball while disallowing the progression of the opponent.

Coaching on Principles

21/02/2020

Yesterday I received an email from a PhD student regarding the "Principles". His question was regarding the way coaches apply the principles into our daily practise, how we do it and how we achieve player understanding of the game. This is what his question produced. I hope you find it interesting.

How can we achieve a certain level of coordination between the decision-making of 11 different players inside the field? How can we develop an intelligent game? How do we organize our game principles? And how do players learn them?

If we address the first question, in the theory there are two models that try to explain the behaviour of players from two different perspectives: the cognitive perspective and the dynamical-ecological perspective. I don't want to bother you with long theoretical explanations, so I will be very short and precise:

The Cognitive Perspective assumes that between perception and execution of the action there is a cognitive process. Once a particular situation is given to the player, the player compares it with its mental representation and finds the correct answer, that afterwards is executed. If these mental representations are shared among players, their behaviours will be coordinated due to this shared mental framework of the game.

The Dynamical-Ecological Perspective assumes that between the perception and the action there is not enough time to call a mental representation from the memory. This perspective considers that players are directly perceiving the environment with "opportunities to act" (affordances) attached. These affordances are the content of what we colloquially call intuition. Even from the dynamic-ecological perspective, a previous "learning" of the game is needed. If so, players will become more sensible to certain stimuli and they will tend to find certain information in more relevant parts of the context. Players should understand what is suitable to perceive.

Among academics there is a consensus that both perspectives coexist, and its importance is related to the time available in the decision-making process. If the player has enough time between perception and action, the player can recall mental representations easily. If a player is forced to perceive and execute immediately, here we just have affordances and pure intuition. Both positions are vigent, complementary and constantly cohexiting.

When we achieve an intelligent team, the initiative of each individual is significant for the rest of the team. This initiative is also coherent with the game model and its principles. We need decision-making challenges and constant problem-solving under pressure and various constraints. This is the way our brains develop! In my opinion, a good coach is the one who tries to explain the internal logic of the game, the most convenient principles and what and where are the significant sources of information during the action.

Principles are abstractions. Abstractions that, based on experience, allow us to find commonalities through different situations. These abstractions are ideas that help us to organize and categorize the complex reality. From concrete to generic. Principles not only help us to organize and identify, but also help us to anticipate and to expect, which is crucial during the action. Principles should be organized. They follow a fractal structure. In every principle there is the whole game model contained.

In the process of teaching we should start from the most inclusive principles and then break down the system gradually. This is what is called **"Progressive Differentiation"**. Training tasks should be significant and relevant for our game model acquisition. By significant I mean with a high degree of functionality/transference/ specificity. We need a guide when we play. How we play is a must question to constantly pose. The focus of the training should be clear, we can't pretend that our players consciously develop 10 different principles at the same time. This is what is called **"Sequential Organization"**

In training players should face contradictions between principles as well (bringing them to the zone of proximal development). That conflictive process creates a better understanding of the game logic. Nonetheless, training tasks should be funny and a source of joy. Players shouldn't fail in more than 20% of the cases (the rule

126

of 80/20 is commonly used in dog training and in video game design). If you achieve that, they will be motivated, focused and the predisposition for new learnings will be higher. We shouldn't punish the error. In young players, the fear of losing the ball is so important that they focus all the attention on that. That diminishes the perception of the context, reduces the cognitive resources available and also increases the stress level in the body while jeopardizing motor skills.

The best way to develop our players in game principles is with the use of appropriate Small-Sided where we achieve our desired propentions, so players can often experience the game principles under complex scenarios.

Game is the best coach.

The Philosophy of the Position

08/04/2020

What is the position? The position of what? The position itself? No, the position is always related to an object or subject. For example, it is common to say "my body position is low" or "the position of the book is too high", for example. However, every position needs a frame of reference to become standardized and then meaningful for other observers. For instance, and talking about hockey, if I say, "Andreu is on the right", is that referred to the side of the pitch or to the side of the player? If I say "Andreu is the deepest player of the team", that proposition uses two variables, the pitch and the position of the other team mates. So we see how "positions" can be determined by one or more variables.

Why do we use positions in hockey? Well, the fact that there is only 1 ball and 22 players trying to manipulate it, brings the need of coordination among them. In attack and in defense. This coordination drives the position of players in a particular way.

Long time ago, coaches decided to cope with this need of organizing the positions with a great idea: to assign a singular position to a single player. So, for example: "Andreu, you will play as left defender." These positions were cartesian, in the sense that are referred to two coordinates: the line (Y axis) and the side (X). So we had left defenders, mid mids, right strikers, etc. With this spatial determination, the complexity of the game was reduced, because if players were respecting this spatial assignment, the team was always organized (rationally distributed lengthwise and crosswise of the field). Under this old paradigm that makes no sense to play with two left defenders at the same time or to play without strikers (it goes against its logic).

This cartesian paradigm of positions is vigent today as well. The current tactics take this organization as premise and then build the tactical variations upon it. For example, we can have a right defender who joins the center of the field under certain conditions. But that player IS still a left defender. Indeed, the specific position became an essential attribute of every player. The natural outcome of this paradigm is to have experts in every particular position after playing and training it for a long time. A diversity in positions is seen as a source of inefficiency. Our culture adopted normal questions like: "What's your position"? But answers like "I'm the central defender". So you can see how the player adopts the position as part of his/her self.

Once positions become roles, every player has a different set of skills and behaviours to perform during the game. This set of information depends on the position, so if we change the player, the new substitute should perform the same function. This is the way teams are mostly built, as if they were production lines with different profiles of workers involved. Industrial paradigm. We have seen how position can be related to the field and its coordinates, but can the position be related to other variables? Yes. We can organize the players according to their distance to the ball, for example. So you can have "ball carrier, close, intermediate and distant players". Players will constantly move from one role to another depending on where the ball is. And depending on the adopted role, they will have different preferent behaviours to adopt. It's just a different paradigm. You can imagine many others. They are all valid! You just need to define the criterion of differentiation and then establish functions during the game (game principles).

Can we play without any positional organization of the players? Yes, you can do it. You can play without predefined tactics. And you will see how "positional" sense will naturally emerge from the game. Some players will naturally run close to the ball carrier, some others will stand at the back, some will stand next to the goal. And each of them will follow an internal logic to do that, mostly unconscious. You just have to look at how kids of 10 years old play street hockey. Tactics will always emerge in every game that is played by rational beings.

So do we need to have common tactics? Yes I claim, because without any common system based on positional awareness you will not be able to optimize the interactions between your players. The effective game requires an intelligent use of the space, and for that you need a game model (a set of preferent behaviours). But even a bad plan is better than no plan. The game model tells the players in what position is more significant to stand. Guides the players in occupying certain positions more often than others. Show the players what positions are more dangerous for the opponent than others. The game model takes the whole existent field of possibilities and ponders them according to certain objectives.

We should start thinking about positions but far beyond the way we did it in the past. Position is not an attribute to the player. You are not a defender, my friend, you attack and defend all the time simultaneously. And we will try to help you in doing that better, cause we are artisans, not industrials.

Positions are just the necessary conditions of our tactical principles. We can't coordinate ourselves effectively if we're not located right.

The position is in our game model, not in ourselves.

PLAYERS

10 Habits of Successful Hockey Players

14/02/2018

I want to summarize what, in my honest opinion, are the most important qualities that any successful player should possess in contemporary hockey. I want to do it in a "top10" format. I will try to exemplify every habit with the example of some real role models. All of them men (due to my former player experience). I've been lucky to "suffer" most of them inside the field, so I'm able to speak with full knowledge in this case.

Maximize your V/P ratio: In average, a hockey player is in contact with the ball around 2' per game. Out of these two minutes, the player should spend as much time as possible with the vision enabled. That means to attend the environment instead of the ball. We can split this attention into two types: full vision (where the focus of the attention is "out there" and the ball is controlled through intuition/expertise) or peripheral vision (where the focus of the attention is around the ball but with a peripheral field of vision enabled). Good players are always able to put the attention "out there" and increase the ratio vision/possession. Bad players live "down here" with the ball. Players like Hauke, Kemperman, Oliva, Mazzilli, Van Doren or Stanzl are good examples of this mastery in vision.

Kill your opponent with accelerations: During the game every defender faces a fundamental dilemma: what to do when the binomial "player-ball" is broken. In that moment 95% of the defenders decide to follow the ball and lose the presence of the attacker. If this attentional omission is exploited by the attacker with the use of a proper acceleration that will generate a window of advantage for a while. This is the essence of the "give and go", for example. Accelerations can also be used in "third-man" combinations, overlaps or just in 1v1 duels. But let's be clear: there is no possible generation of advantage without wise accelerations. Teun de Nooijer was the first master in this skill. And after him we had many other dutch players like Robert van der Horst or Valentin Verga following his pathway. Nowadays this is already a common denominator among top players. A *sine qua non* condition if you want to excel.

Be an expert in the art of deception: wise, shrewd, bold, delusive... These "dark" skills are mostly (but not only) learned through experience. If you want to perform above others you should be able to deceive or mislead if needed. I'm talking about body fakes, vision fakes, verbal fakes, but also about the wise use of the rules to frustrate your rivals. On this topic, the greatest master I have ever seen was Carlos Retegui. During the game he was able to control his teammates, the opponents, the umpires, both benches, the spectators of both teams and even the ball-boys. What a genius!

Aggressiveness is not negotiable: hockey is becoming more and more physical. Physical contact will be more accepted and tolerated by the umpires. In hockey we know that goals can only be scored inside the circle. That rule generates a "highly transcendent" field of battle for both teams, attackers and defenders. Inside the circles every inch and every instant of time has an enormous value. It's worth fighting hard for it. Never be violent, but be very aggressive and never refuse the contact. For example, I love how Mirco Pruyser bravely uses his body inside the D. There are other super aggressive role model players like Teun Rohof, Sergi Enrique, Juan Martin Lopez or Glenn Turner. These players are always welcome in your team, and most of the time they are hated by the opponents.

All good defenders got a Master in Risk Assessment: In field hockey, where the physical contact is very penalized, to steal a ball without committing fault is a mastery about risk management. The distance from where to put pressure, not too far, not too close. The speed of your stick movement during interceptions and jabs. The proper timing about how to tackle. The wisdom in the use of shavings. The footwork while defending a full speed attacker. How to find doubles. How to defend inside the circle. How to use "smooth collision" faults to prevent circle entries. As you can see there is a fine line between being an expert in defense and being a ruthless fault machine. In my opinion, one of the best defenders in risk assessment is Matias Rey: elegance, intelligence, and effortless efficiency.

Be Multifunctional!: In contemporary hockey we don't have "specialized" players anymore. We need players that can understand the fundamentals of the game and then be able to play in any part of the field. No more defenders, midfielders or strikers. This Cartesian scheme is becoming obsolete. Do you want to know who's more multifunctional? Imagine 11 Mats Grambusch playing against 11 Tom Grambusch. Both super players! But the question is which team would win. In the long run multifunctional players will dominate the world. It is already happening.

"Give me the ball": When things get ugly top players make a step forward and try to change the course of the events by themselves. They automatically enhance their presence inside the field. They start to irradiate energy, encourage teammates, manage the tempo of the game and participate more often. They want to bring the game back under their rule, and they do it while having the ball. I've seen this "heroic" capacity in very few players, but Santi Freixa and Moritz Fürste were amazing examples.

Develop your game sense: There is nothing worse than a motivated fool. Most of the top players are smart in the interpretation of the game. They are a little bit like coaches inside the field. Your tactical sense will be the base for your decision making. The decisions you take should be the appropriate ones according to the tactical principles of your team. Is it time to launch a fast break or it is better to keep control? Should I play a quick restart after this free hit or should I wait? Is it better to play long or short passing? Should I run the line over line movement or should I stand in guard position? These are some of the micro tactical decisions that must be constantly taken by players. If you repeatedly fail in your choices your talent will be useless for the team. Examples of intelligent players: Mark Knowles, Barry Middleton or Arthur Van Doren.

Slaps with one hand, caresses with the other: Top players are powerful. As Machiavelli said, power is a balance between love and fear. Love? Yes, be admired and inspire others. Try to make them better. Take care of everyone and be able to create joy within the group. But also be respected. Put people in tension if the situation requires it. Your words must be followed. Punish if needed. Forge discipline and fight hard against toxicity. Slaps and caresses. In the Spanish national team we had Rodrigo Garza playing this role. Martin Häner can be another example.

Kaizen Attitude: It may sound a cliché, but it's never too late to learn new things and improve your performance. Try new things and benchmark others. Learn from different athletes, from other sports if needed. Be critical with your coach and demand more and better resources for your growth. Take care of your health. Keep your head in the stars but your feet on the ground. When I see veteran players like Paredes, Gilardi, Vivaldi, Quemada, Cortès, Knowles, etc, what I see is not the triumph of talent but the success of humility and hard work.

The Ontology of Passing

16/04/2018

Yesterday, after drinking a couple of wine glasses I started to reflect about "what is a pass" and what makes a pass something desirable in team sports like field hockey. Some chaotic ideas came into my mind. It was a kind of magic insight, like the ones from the mathematician Ramanujan, but sponsored by Dionysus in my case.

First of all, when we use the term "pass", what do we mean? It is referred to the pathway traveled by the ball from player to player. Passes can be short, long, flat, aerial, frontward, backward, soft, hard, deliberate, blind...this type of categorization is something that we won't address in the present text.

Let's suppose that we play hockey and as an umpire I fix a new rule that states that passes are not allowed anymore. What would the game look like? The game would be something like a permanent succession of 1v1 transitions between different players. What is the origin of the 1st pass in hockey history? The discovery of the 1st pass took place due to the need to avoid the defender and progress towards the goal with less resistance. **The pass was invented as a vehicle to eliminate opponents from direct opposition** and to bring the ball into an easier context.

Then, why do we pass the ball backward? Passing the ball backward (so going further from our target!) should be something stupid, right? No. It's not stupid, but there is another reason why we pass the ball: **we pass the ball to avoid a risk of loss and secure the ball possession**. When the resistance applied by the opponent is complex perhaps the only space to progress is far away from our position and it requires an intermediate back pass for the consequent transfer and then progression.

(TIP: Design a small-sided game where backward passes are only allowed inside the circle. Great fun, like India-Pakistan during the 90's!)

Every passing line can be disabled by defenders. The defender is like a wall, in this sense. The Defender possesses an imaginary influence area in which he/she can move the stick and intercept the ball if required. This wall influence area is -due to the nature of our sport- asymmetric. Being bigger on the right-hand side of the defender. The ratio between the size of this coverage area and the size of the ball is a crucial factor to analyze. For example, in football the ball is so big in relation with the two legs of the defender. In hockey the ball is smaller and we can only use the stick to stop it (the foot is offence). The success of the defender in interceptions is so dependent on the reaction speed and distance from the ball carrier. The closer the defender is from the passer, less is the time to react and activate the body for the movement of interception. Therefore, **in hockey the elimination pass should be taken as much closer to the defender as possible.**

A passing line is open when there is no possible interception between the passer and the receiver. This is what I call an enlightened pass. A pass that can take place in the light. Defenders are objects to avoid and, due to their physical presence, generate a shadow area behind them. Within these dark trails passes can't be completed because there is an obstacle in between passer and receiver: the defender. Do you want to receive the ball? Escape from the shadow and enter to the light, where the elighted pass can be completed. This is the fundamental logic of the "stick to stick" principle.

Inside a hockey field we have 22 players looking at the same object: the hockey ball. When the defender is engaged by the attacker the attention is directed into the ball. Our field of vision is around 210º width. Out of this 210º, 80º are part of the peripheral vision (approximately 40º per side). Peripheral vision is imprecise and vague. Taking this vision factor into our equation we can differentiate between passes that cross and break the field of vision of the defender and the passes that occur within the same field of vision of the defender. For example, if there is a pass in front of me and I just have to slightly turn my head in order to follow the ball, this pass doesn't break my field of vision. But if the pass is a vertical aerial that forces me to turn completely in order to follow the pathway of the ball, this pass has crossed and broken my field of vision. Ok, let's keep this in mind for now.

Previously we stated that the closer the ball is from the defender, the bigger is the dark trail so less passing options remain open for the attacker. In football, the opposition from the defender is solid because the ball is big and the defender can block it with both legs (that is the reason why the "panna" is so spectacular, because of its difficulty). Therefore, in football the passes must be completed around the defender, not through him. But when passes are travelling far around the defender, the body turn that the defender is forced to do, in order to track the ball, is smaller and easier. That is the reason why tiki-taka is only successful when it is executed within 1 or 2 touches maximum. The ball has to travel quicker than the field of vision of the defenders.

But hockey is different. The opposition from defenders is vulnerable because the stick and ball are small objects. And also because every ball that touches the foot represents a contingency award for the attacker. In hockey, the closer we are to the defender, more vulnerable he becomes because the time-reaction for the ball interception decreases. Metaphorically, defenders in hockey allow more light rays to go through as they become proximal to the ball carrier.

But that's not all. These passes are also violent crosses that halve the field of vision of the defender. After one of these "elimination passes" if the defender wants to recuperate the visual contact with the ball, the defender has to completely turn his body. But there is still another extra advantage of using these elimination passes: when defender is crossed by the ball and is forced to turn his field of vision loses the presence of the passer, while leaving that player into a "new dark" area. This indirect oblivion allows the former passer the chance to become the receiver of a new hypothetical pass. That is the fundamental logic of the "give and go" principle.

In hockey, the best passes are those that cross the field of vision of the defender and those that travel through the shadow influence area. **Therefore, the closer we can be from the defender in the moment of passing, the better.**

It's all about bringing light to the darkness.

Scoring Goals as a Process

07/05/2018

If you want to win, just score more goals than your opponent. That stupid and obvious statement derives in two lines of thought, first one: you should try to avoid goals from your opponent (defense) and second: you should try to score goals (attack). Without conceding goals against you can't lose. But without scoring goals you can't win. This is the fundamental philosophical dilemma in the core of any game strategy. How to manage these two pulsations in order to optimize your results is what makes coaching so complex.

The present text is about scoring goals, not about defending. In my opinion, the way we approach the phenomenon "goal" is too simplistic. A field goal is a complex event, always a result of multiple and non-linear interactions. Something unpredictable by its nature. Therefore, it is something that is more difficult to train than just motivating the strikers and organizing a couple of shooting drills. However, the fact that the "goal" is complex doesn't mean that we can't analyze it deeply and find some guidelines and properties that can make us maximize the probability to score.

Let's go step by step. According to our rules and regulations, you can't score a goal without having the possession inside the opponent's circle. In a standard hockey match every team has around 60 possessions. These 60 possessions have a beginning and an end. For example, one of your outlets starts in your ¼ and ends up in the ¾ of the field. But you can also have a high recovery after a good press in opposite ¾ and finalize that possession with a circle penetration. The higher you finalize your possessions the closer you will be from the circle. If your team usually recovers the possession low in the field, you need either long fast breaks or a very effective vertical progression. If your team recovers high on the field, you just need to perform your short counter-attacks. If you recover high it's easier to reach the opposite circle (but we all know how difficult it is to recover high in the field).

Out of 60 possessions, around 50% of them end up inside, at least, opponent's ¼. This is the first step in our goal scoring process: track and maximize the number of possessions ending in opponent's ¼. If we are below 50%, we're a bit further of the "scoring a goal" event. If we're above 50%, our scoring process starts well. *Coach challenge: how can we have more ¼ entries out of our total number of possessions?*

Let's focus on those 30 possessions per game in opponent's ¼,. Out of these 30 entries, around 50% use to finalize inside the circle. That means around 16 circle penetrations per game. This is an average number that can be used at any level. If you're above 16 fine! If not, problematic! *Coaches challenge: how can we transform our ¼ possessions into more circle penetrations?*

Out of 16 circle penetrations per game, 50% turn into a goal attempt.

This category includes a shot on target (SOT) or an award of PC. That means around 8 goal chances per game. Once the ball is inside the circle players should focus on how to generate the "goal attempt" ,not the goal yet. The objective must be the SOT (or to get a PC if you're in a narrow-angle spot). Here what is important is to have players that are able to send the ball towards the goal post. Especially considering that most of the field goals are scored inside the 7m circle. That must be the focus, not scoring yet, I insist. This is the step where we commonly face most of the troubles. *Coaches challenge: how can we convert our circle penetrations into more goal chances?*

If there is an average of 8 goal attempts per game. Around 4 will be PC's and the other 4 will be SOT. Out of 4 PCs, you should be able to score, at least 1 (25% effectiveness is standard). Out of 4 SOT's you should be able to score, at least 2 (50% effectiveness is normal). *Coaches Challenge: how can we convert our SOT's into goals? If you're below 50%, that means that you should put the focus into goal shooting (with variability please!). If you're above you're lucky! And the same for PC effectiveness.* 3 is the average number of goals that are scored per game.

Deconstructing the goal into a succession of interrelated events and KPI's, like we did here, can easily help us to identify the weak spots of our attack and, if properly trained, improve the odds to score more goals per game. Have you ever tracked these numbers in your team? That is a good way to know more about how your team functions.

But at the end scoring goals will remain a complex phenomenon and maximizing odds will never mean automatic victories, especially in the short-run. This is the magic of our sport and the nightmare for us coaches!

The Copernican Revolution

26/09/2018

The present text aims to approach the crucial role of "vision" in team sports. In our case in field hockey where besides the opponent and the ball there is also an implement to manage. Hockey can be considered a very demanding sport that requires complex motor skills to effectively dominate the ball with the stick. That technical difficulty requires a lot of visual attention from the practitioner.

There's a lot written about vision in sports. Here I just want to highlight the most important vision qualities that should be improved: contrast sensitivity, dynamic visual acuity, monocular and binocular vision (non-dominant eye), visual fusion flexibility, perception of depth, manual-eye coordination, improvements in visual anticipation, reaction time, peripheral vision and kinesthetic control. As we can see vision performance is a broad field of work! However, the goal of this text is not to explain how to practise these qualities. What I want here is to point out what represents the most important "turn" if we talk about vision in field hockey.

There is a consensus among coaches about the importance of vision in field hockey. Coaches from all over the world are constantly demanding "scanning" to their players. To scan means to be aware of your context. "Blind" players are not able to play well because they don't have enough perceptions to feed and optimize their decision-making process. The problem is that we are wrong in the way we approach this "scanning" skill.

What we normally do is to explain that while carrying the ball players must switch between head-up and head down. Head up in order to see the environment and head down in order to control the ball. So the attention goes sequentially from the ball to the context, and from the context to the ball again. The ocular movements used in this sequence of head movements are called "saccadic movements". The saccadic movements are used to detect objects that are outside our central vision. When we detect an object through our peripheral vision then we move our head and eyes and we put ourselves in a position where that desired object can be now detected through our central vision. The problem of using saccadic movements in field hockey is the vertical angle between the ball (head-down) and the context (head-up). A big vertical angle is the worst scenario for the saccadic movements because our field of vision is wider than higher. In other words, if we would be able to carry the ball in our hands instead than on the field, the scenario would be much better. But under our hockey circumstances, the precision of these saccadic movements are poor and not efficient.

Beyond the poor rendiment of saccadic movements. The sequential pattern of "head-up/head-down" also makes it more difficult for a good decision making during the game. The justification is simple: if I'm "open" (head-up) to my teammates intermittently, then the odds to connect with others are reduced because an eventual connexion between passer and receiver would only take place when my open vision matches the lead timing of my teammate.

Other coaches are teaching something a bit different to players: the importance of carrying the ball in front of the body, so the player can put the attention to the ball but at the same time, through peripheral vision, detect part of the environment. Warning! That is also wrong. The problem with this skill is the nature of peripheral vision, which is very poor in chromatic sensitivity and visual acuity. However, the peripheral vision is super sensitive to movement detection. So we will detect opponents, but then we will have to execute a saccadic movement in order to know exactly what that visual stimulus is. And then we face the same problem that we faced earlier.

The authentic revolution takes place when the player becomes able to carry the ball without the need to see it. The revolution is to be able to keep the control of the ball while feeling it. The Copernican turn is to trust our kinesthetic feeling instead of trusting our eyes. Kinesthesis is the consciousness of our body position and our movements. If we feel the ball well then we can fully employ our vision resources into the environment.

This motor skill requires time and practise. If you look at the best players, they do it quite often (mixing this kinesthetic control with peripheral vision and saccadic movements). But one thing is clear: the more time we can keep our vision enabled with the ball under control, better tactical decisions we will be able to take. The player will feel that it is placed "out there". There is no subject-object duality. Passing lines will be drawn in real-time and the connexions with receivers will become subtle and fine. With your head-up you become an artist inside the field. The *übermensch*.

> *The better that we feel the ball, the more we can see the field. The more we see the field, the better decisions we can take. The better decisions we take, the better players we become. And the better players you are able to develop, the better coach you are.*

The problem of running too much

27/12/2018

How many times have you criticized one of your players for being too static inside the field? "Coach, I'm not touching the ball enough," he claims. "So run more", you respond. Why? Why do we believe that running is intrinsically desirable in hockey? The more we run, the better we play?

Everything started with the unlimited-substitutions rule. That rule was famously exploited by the Germans under Bernhard Peters. The rule allowed dozens of interchanges (around 60 subs per game) instead of the previous three. The possibility to constantly interchange our players created a big change in the running taxonomy of our sport (together with the self-pass rule, later on). More meters per minute and distances covered at a higher pace. That phenomenon has been transferred into the game with the appearance of higher intensities, more transitions and a more direct style of play.

Players know that they will have some sets of 6 minutes to play and 3 minutes of rest in between. During these 6 minutes they try to give everything they can! They run a lot in ball possession as well as in defense. Australia in 2014 was the paradigmatic example of that. Full-press all the time, ball press in defensive transitions, massive withdrawals and quick counters, fast breaks, direct play, etc. They ran more meters at higher intensities than others. And after their success they established the standard. This physical credo is still impregnating our hockey today. Unfortunately, because this mantra of "the importance of running" hides the essential. I will try to explain why running has no intrinsic value itself. Running should not be considered a relevant KPI. And I'll try to go forward while claiming that most of the time running is even counterproductive.

Hockey is a game. You PLAY hockey. To play means to participate. To actively participate. When you're on the field you want to actively participate in the game. And in hockey that means touching the ball. Normally, the more you participate the better you feel. That is true for everyone, from my 9-years-old nephew to the Belgium international players.

The longer I'm inside the field, the more odds to participate and therefore to feel happy. The less time I'm inside, less odds. Common sense. But if I play in short periods of time and I'm full of energy when I do it, then I will try to run as much as possible before "my time" ends because I want to maximize my active participation. Simple logic, right?

And this is how players become anxious of participation and recognition. Recognition yes: I am a player when I play, when I participate. Players run because they believe that "running maximizes the odds to participate". When the anxious player finally receives the ball, he's stressed and full of energy. Then what does he do? He protects the precious treasure and runs to space. Any associative intention implies a risk of loss, and he doesn't want to commit any mistake. First he wants to enjoy the possession of the ball. He wants to taste the sweet participation. Very primitive feeling but totally understandable, given these circumstances.

Some players run too quickly. When the ball is carried too quickly and under stress, the quality of the contact stick-ball diminishes. The ball is carried through touches instead of through permanent contact. With touches the ball demands more attention from the player and therefore vision becomes sequential ball-context-ball-context. That constant head and eye movement hinders the capacity to perceive the environment and therefore, the capacity to connect with other potential receivers. Decision-making process is jeopardized because the carrying technique is not appropriate. The carrying technique is not appropriate because the player is too excited. The player is too excited because he was anxious to participate.

What are the common outcomes of these actions? Our player misses the pass or protects the ball again and gives it backwards. In both cases he feels frustration because the meritorious participation was not accomplished. He goes back to the bench again, reflecting on the previous mediocre actions and waiting for the next entry where he will have another short chance to demonstrate his value. And anxiety grows again.

There is something worse than a player who is too anxious to participate: a player who is scared to participate. You can detect these players because they also run too much, but they always run far from the ball. You can't lose any ball if you don't touch it. Coaches, if you detect one of these players, death by hanging is the right measure to take.

The process that we've seen is built on a wrong understanding of the game, which is: the more you run, the more you participate. This fallacy is still vigent in most hockey minds. Most of the players believe that "to lead" is "to move", therefore "to run". So these players spend most of the time running all over the field. They run and run while trying to escape from the opponent. But that doesn't work. The opponent is always behind. The player feels frustration because the resource "run" doesn't allow more receivings, so they try it harder and run more. Fail. So what players should do in order to participate more and better? Messi, don't lose the faith in us, illuminate us!

Well, precisely starting with the opposite: the quieter you are the better. Stand still and try to surprise your opponent with accelerations. Like the hunter does. The acceleration is part of the communicative act between both players, the passer and the receiver. As Menotti wisely said: *"You know that when I go then I come, and when I come then I go."*

It's about smart accelerations. On the right occasion of time and space. Acceleration with and without the ball. Accelerations to surprise and fakes to manipulate. Good players don't run too much. Good players interact well with other teammates. Successful accelerations require this relational capacity between individuals. Understanding when, where and how to move. The connecting capital of a player is his ability to effectively connect with others inside the field. The better connected that you can be with your teammates, the more chances to participate and better participation you'll provide to your team.

As coaches we should primarily attend this connecting capital of our players. Try to develop that. Don't be dazzled with individual actions, dribblings and long runs. Pay more attention to what they haven't seen than to what they have done. Pay attention to misunderstandings, confusions and disconnections between them, because these are the crucial indicators to follow.

"Run less but run better"

Synergies

01/07/2019

Do you remember how Dani Alves and Leo Messi were able to combine between each other? If so, you remember a very good example of what is called "bilateral synergy" (also called "society"). Remember the wise use of the 1st-touch passes, the non verbal communication, the perfect changes of pace, fakes...These types of societies are rare and precious. In football as well as in hockey. And when we find one like that one, we automatically fall in love for its beauty and harmony.

Synergies are defined as functional groups of elements that act as a sole coherent unity (J.A. Scott Kelso). These synergies are based upon the principle of auto-organization. This principle enables players to find effective and efficient solutions in complex changing environments, but spontaneously, that is without commands or sets of instructions. Indeed, Alves and Messi are not forced to play like that. It is not due to the coach that they connect like they do. However, the fact that "societies" emerge by themselves, does it mean that we can't make them flourish in our team? No, I don't think so.

There are players with more "connecting capital" than others. Normally strikers are the ones with less capacity to interrelate, and that is basically for two reasons: Since youth they were responsible and judged for scoring goals, not for assisting or playing nice combinations with other teammates. And secondly, the most intelligent players (best decision makers) in youth ages are spotted in the midfield or in the center of the defense as player makers, never as strikers.

So, what can we do? First of all, be aware of cues and subtle signs from the players. Check if there are already natural attractors between your players. Look when they play, try to detect how often they relate with each other but also the quality of this relation. Do they need an obvious and easy context to connect? Or is it something subtle and intuitive? Are these connections erratic or they follow certain patterns? Are these two players sharing a common style of play? Are they enjoying themselves when they combine?

Once a significant society is detected then it has to be enhanced. Significant is an important adjective. It has to be significant (there are tangible returns) and good for the team and for the global performance. So, once detected, make sure that these two players play close to each other inside the field and give them freedom to exploit combinations. Make them converge. Put them together during the week (Messi and Alves were always warming up together), sharing a team during training. The more time they spend together, the stronger the sinergy will be. Recognize and empower them. Publicly and explicitly.

The last step takes place when this society is widely accepted and valued inside the squad. That happens when the style of the synergy is coherent and compatible with the style of the team. Once more players start sharing the same game style, synergies will emerge more often and between more players. This is the best thing that FCBarcelona achieved: to form a unique style of play since youth ages. A common way to understand each other inside the field. It was not only Messi and Alves who connected well, also Xavi, Busquets, Piqué, Iniesta, Alba, Fábregas, Pedro and many other "Masia" boys.

Nothing is more beautiful than a good passing combination!

Combinations with the 3rd

14/01/2020

"The third man is impossible to defend, impossible ... I'll explain what it means. Imagine Piqué wanting to play with me, but I'm marked, I have a marker (defender) on me, a very aggressive guy. Well, it is clear that Piqué can not pass it to me, it is evident. If I move away, I'll take the marker with me. Then, Messi goes down and becomes the second man. Piqué is the 1st, Messi the 2nd and I the 3rd. I have to be very alert, right?! Piqué, then plays with the 2nd man, Messi, who returns it, and at that moment I'm an option. I'm now free of my marker who has moved to defend closer to the ball. Now I'm totally unmarked and Piqué passes me the ball. If my marker is looking at the ball, cannot see that I'm unmarked and then I appear, I'm the third man. We have already achieved superiority(...)" Xavi Hernández (extracted from the book "Senda de Campeones" from Martí Perarnau).

Here we had an explanation about the "Third Man" (now "3M") by Xavi Hernandez, the former FCBarcelona midfielder and probably one of the most iconic players of this "tiki-taka" style of play. This tactical concept or principle is very important in football, especially for clubs who want to play a good "positional" style of play like FCB. The aim of positional game is to find and generate superiorities through smart use of locations and passes.

In hockey, these 3M combinations already exist but are rare to see compared to football. The Netherlands is a good ambassador of this movement. They call it "1-3's". The aim of this text is to convince more coaches about its potential (impossibility to be defended) and the importance to enhance its knowledge and its use by the players. The success of the 3M is due to six reasons:

1) The defender's impulse to close the center

Defenders want to close the center, that is a common principle in defense for most of the teams. Therefore, when defenders mark an opponent, they will always do it from the "inside", that is, from the side that is closer to the goal line. And if they can, they will try to be closer to the ball (to have the chance of interception). That positioning is what coaches call the "defensive triangle". If well applied, the attacker has very few chances to eliminate the defender or receive the ball in a good positioning. So yes, for a good 3M combination, we need a very good defender who is doing its job perfectly and prevents the pass between two players.

2) The limitation of the human field of vision

With our two eyes we have slightly more than 180 degrees of field of vision. That limited field of vision automatically generates a "dark" zone behind us. A zone where we obviously can't detect objects. This is the zone to exploit by the 3M, the zone behind the direct defender's vision. When covered, Instead of fighting to get the space against this good defender, the attacker should accept the initial defeat and wait wisely for the chance to exploit the "dark" side.

3) The impossibility to prevent the post-up

Every defender knows that anticipation becomes something impossible when your opponent decides to quickly lead downwards towards the ball. As a defender you always stay behind, but that is fine because you're always closer to the goal than your opponent. And if the attacker receives in front of you and turns, you're always there ready to defend.

4) The seduction of the ball

The ball seduces the players. The ball has a magic magnetism that attracts everyone's attention. Inside the field, players always follow the ball and direct their vision into the small object. The magical aspect of this fact is that when defenders follow the path of the ball, they totally forget the presence of other objects, including their marks. And that is especially interesting when that forgotten attacker becomes spotted into the dark zone. The ball attracts the defender's attention and liberates the attacker, who is now ready to be the 3M.

5) The limitation of the human reaction time

It's around 0,5" (depending on many factors), but there is always reaction time. Defenders react, so they are always a bit late. When the pass between the ball carrier and the post-up takes place, our 3M, who has just been liberated, starts an acceleration forward. When the defender identifies that the ball has been played vertically, he naturally drops back, but when he realizes that his previous mark has accelerated, it's already too late to catch him.

6) The quick delivery

That vertical pass reaches the post-up player, who is also seeing the 3M progressing towards him, free of opposition and in positional superiority as well (defender behind). The post-up should quickly drop the ball to the 3M. The 3M receives that ball facing the attack, on the move and ready to exploit the superiority.

Due to these 6 reasons I say that 3M combinations are really difficult to defend. But these types of combinations are very difficult to implement. A smart movement of three players requires a high level of coordination. And that is something difficult to achieve. You need a lot of good coaching and good training tasks in order to build this connection between your players.

Note: In this text I've used the denomination "Third-Man" as it's widely used all over the sports world. However, and in order to avoid any gender discrimination, the concept should be named "Playing with the 3rd", "Finding the 3rd" or just "1-3".

The Etymology of Winning

26/04/2020

Etymology is the history of the words. The archeology of the language. The mission of the present article is to prepare an etymological review about the concepts "win" and "victory". The goal of this text is to better and wider understand their meaning and explore how we can use this semantic-time-travel to get a deeper knowledge of these two big topics. Probably the utility of this article will tend to zero. But I'm not sure if value always means utility. The starting point can be the search of the current official definitions. According to Cambridge Dictionary (it sounds reliable):

- Win: to achieve first position and/or get a prize in a competition, election, fight, etc

- Victory: an occasion when you win a game, competition, election, war, etc. or the fact that you have won.

Clear. There is a zero sum contest where one agent prevails above the other. Now I will try to show how etymology can bring us further and deeper into that. A journey through the planet and history. Let's start.

The word *"win"* comes from the old english *"winnan"*, this term is referred to labour, toil, struggle, rage, oppose, resist... Here we can see how in the essence of these "winning processes" we always have to overcome certain opposition, therefore the need to persist and fight. That's important for us. There is no costless victory. We always have to invest something (pay the price!). There is an inherent struggle in winning.

"Winnan" comes from the old Proto-Indo-European (PIE) root *"wenh"* (to strive, wish, desire, love). Things get more interesting here. What can we learn? The object of the contest must be something desirable for us. We will be ready to resist in the game only if we love what we do. Only if we desire to win. Winning and loving are deeply related!

From *"wehn"* derives the term *"Venus"*, the roman goddess of love. We should pray to Venus if we want to win our beloved man, woman or trophy!. *"Venerate"* also derives from the same root. To venerate is to treat with great respect. To love. But also the word *"venom"*, and yes, we all know how harmful can be the loss when we don't achieve the desired goal.

Let's talk about "victory" now. From the latin *"victoria"* and *"vincere"*: (to conquer, to overcome) and from the PIE root *"weyk"*, a broad root that drives us to a broad variety of meanings. First of all, *"weyk"* refers to clan and social unit. Vikings and villa! So here we have the first "social" component of the victory. When we win, we conquer something that benefits us. Something that makes us better as a community. But *"weik"* is also related to bend, to curve. vicissitudes, weakness, wicker. What can we extract from these terms? The vulnerability that we're assuming when we compete. We are subjected to our opponent's will as well. We can be manipulated, submitted and weakened by others. That's the risk. *"Weik"* has also another field of meaning that is related to the fight and to conquer. Invictus, Victor and victory of course are derived words, but also "convince" and "evince". That brings me to the next etymological coaching lesson: by using our arguments and our behaviour, if we achieve a change in others, we are winning the most important contest: to walk the same pathway, and that's one of the most important victories we can achieve as coaches.

But there is still another PIE root that can guide us in our special learning journey. It is the root *"gwey"* (to live, to conquer). From this old root we find -among some others- the interesting sanskrit concept of *"jáyati"* and *"jitá"* (both related to victory and triumph). Today, In Hindi "jai" means victory (Jai Hind!), but also means long life, glory, rejoice, bravo… That shows how joy is also an inherent part of the process of winning. To win rejuvenates us! Probably we wouldn't be as committed as we are if there is no chance to celebrate and enjoy the sweet fruit of the victory once achieved.

In chinese, to win is *"yíng"*, this word comes from the middle chinese /jiɛŋ/ (full, to have surplus, filled) and the old chinese /*leŋ/. I could not find any evidence of connection between the proto-indo-european roots of "wehn", "weyk" and "gwey" and the old chinese /*leŋ/ (at least I could not find it). But they don't look so different, right? Who knows!

I like this materialistic approach of victory. We get or we lose something from the competition. if we win, we finish with a surplus, with an excess that we extracted from our opponent. We feel totally fulfilled. That idea brings me to the concept of *"gain"* (which comes from the old french *"gaigner"*, today *gagner* in french and *ganar* in spanish. And you know what? both terms mean *"win"*). Win is a gain, we all agree on that!

In the Tractatus, Wittgenstein states: "The limits of my language are the limits of my world". Our world becomes bigger if we go deeper into the words.

EPILOGUE

Heraclitus River

"No man ever steps in the same river twice, for it's not the same river and he is not the same man". Heraclitus.

You can always learn something. You can always go deeper, further and beyond. You can always try to approach something from a new perspective. You can always think about doing something different. There is no single truth, nothing fixed, no clarity out there. There are no certainties, nothing solid enough to build upon. Actually, there is nothing such a "you", because you are also constantly changing and so your opinions and views as well. We will never understand hockey enough either, because hockey is constantly changing too. It is impossible to know something if both subject and object are always changing. So you can never learn anything. You can step into the river, but never into the same river. That is the paradox, the learning as an undefined activity.

We are all Sisyphus in the process of achieving something that is inherently impossible to be achieved. But it is precisely that stupid inclination towards the knowledge and the process of learning what brings meaning to our life, what constitute us as humans.

Keep pushing, keep learning.

Andreu Enrich

07/05/2020

THANK YOU!

Thank you for the time you spent reading "Hockey. A Philosophical Game". If you liked this book and found it useful I would be very grateful if you leave your opinion in Amazon. It will help me continue to write books associated to this topic. Your support is very important. I read all the opinions and try to give feedback to make this book better. If you want to contact me, this is my email:

andreu.enrich@gmail.com

Printed in Great Britain
by Amazon